DRINK *like a* LOCAL

LONDON

Drink Like a Local: London
A Field Guide to London's Best Bars

13-Digit ISBN: 978-1-64643-299-8
10-Digit ISBN: 1-64643-299-1

This book may be ordered by mail from the publisher. Please include $5.99 for postage and handling. Please support your local bookseller first!

Books published by Cider Mill Press Book Publishers are available at special discounts for bulk purchases in the United States by corporations, institutions, and other organizations. For more information, please contact the publisher.

Cider Mill Press Book Publishers
"Where good books are ready for press"
PO Box 454
12 Spring Street
Kennebunkport, Maine 04046

cidermillpress.com

Typography: Ballinger, Condor, Pacifico, Poppins, Stolzl

Printed in China

1 2 3 4 5 6 7 8 9 0
First Edition

DRINK *like a* LOCAL
LONDON

*A Field Guide to
London's Best Bars*

FELIPE SCHRIEBERG

CIDER MILL
PRESS

BOOK
PUBLISHERS
KENNEBUNKPORT, MAINE

CONTENTS

This book was written as Britons were just beginning to emerge, relearning how to hang out and relax among large groups of strangers. While most bars and pubs survived the Covid pandemic, sadly, in London and across the United Kingdom, many have permanently shuttered, fatally wounded by the economic damage from the disease. Others managed to hang on and some enterprising and/or crazy individuals even managed to start new bar projects despite strict government restrictions on what they can and cannot do. As these rules are now being lifted, Londoners are eagerly returning to the bars they loved, visiting others they've sought to patronize, and discovering exciting new spaces to enjoy a drink.

So, given this setting, what does it mean to "drink like a local" in London? Certainly not what it meant a few years ago. In the relatively recent past, top bars were creating theatrical, over-the-top, decorative drinks. Any respectable bartender would show off flair moves. Rare sights these days.

Now, a bartender's knowledge of ingredients and mixology, as well as their dedication to good service, is prized above all. Fewer bars rely on the creative gimmicks that drove crowds to them. Only those that also maintained high standards of drinks and service are still around.

Londoners have a few criteria for the bars they choose to frequent. Let's start with the "local": a place near home that they can count on to serve a good drink, offer a space where they relax after work, and even to serve as a place to kick off a big night out on short notice.

The general rule of a genuine Londoner is that she or he should have one pub and one cocktail bar that fits the description above to ensure flexibility, depending on mood and company. That explains in part why top-quality cocktail bars can be found in unusual places in this city—neighborhood clientele will be ready to support it, and regularly.

However, something should be said for novelty. Part of the fun of being in London is keeping track of what's new and great—and discovering the next big thing. Bars that harness this motivation likely will be packed with customers. A decade ago, the trend favored "secret" speakeasy venues, but now it's an innovative approach to making drinks that's the bigger draw. Whatever the reason, the trick is then to make that initial success last over time.

Finally, Londoners enjoy feeling like they've discovered a special secret that they can share (or brag about) with friends—especially when their discovery combines novelty and reliability. I think this is why, excluding some of the superb luxury hotel bars, so many top boozing establishments in London actually are low-key and informal places to hang out. When people can relax, they're in a better frame of mind to enjoy a quality drink—and that's when they will boast about it to their friends (and post about it on social media).

It also makes life easier for those behind the bar who, for the most part, would rather focus both on the quality of their drinks and making sure their customers feel good, rather than create a high-stress or stuffy ambiance.

That commitment to quality applies as well to the many excellent breweries and distilleries that have sprung up in the city over recent years. Almost all small-scale operations offer tours or have taprooms/bars where customers can try their products. This is booze made for Londoners and at a time when consumers are prioritizing local producers, drinking like a London local means discovering and valuing not just bars but booze-makers too.

Advancing a sense of symbiosis in London's booze community, many bars also enjoy serving local beers or using local spirits in their cocktail recipes. Everyone wins.

This book serves not only as a guide to London watering holes but also as a celebration of quality drinks, creativity, and great service at a time, frankly, when we really need it. All the bars mentioned here feature some combination of all three criteria.

It is a pleasure and a privilege to highlight their work, and I hope you'll be able to enjoy a drink or few at some of them soon.

LONDON

CITY OF LONDON

Situated on the original site colonized by the Romans, the City of London is the somewhat confusing name for a district that serves as one of the city's main business hubs. Many legal and financial businesses are based here—and so a healthy number of bars and restaurants have been established to cater to those who work here.

However, during the pandemic this neighborhood was completely deserted—so many of the area's bars had to adapt, re-orient how they do business, or close down. However, the ones listed on the following pages have continued to simply do what they do best.

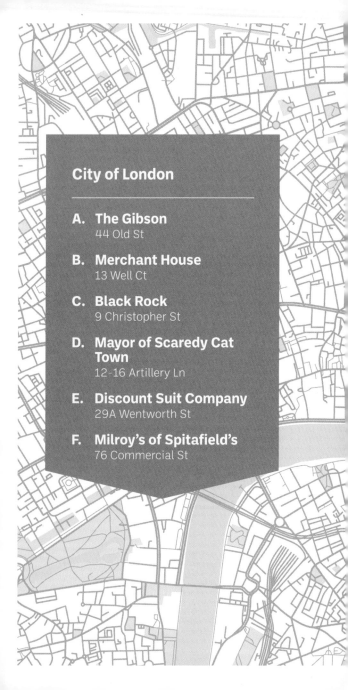

City of London

A. The Gibson
44 Old St

B. Merchant House
13 Well Ct

C. Black Rock
9 Christopher St

D. Mayor of Scaredy Cat Town
12-16 Artillery Ln

E. Discount Suit Company
29A Wentworth St

F. Milroy's of Spitafield's
76 Commercial St

THE GIBSON

44 Old St, London, EC1V 9AQ
Nearest Tube stop: Old Street/Barbican

The Gibson is widely regarded as one of London's heavy hitters when it comes to cocktails. Honoring the time period when the Gibson cocktail was first created in the early twentieth century, the bar's theme could be described as vaguely vintage—a former pub that has been redecorated into something resembling a trendy Edwardian café dominated by a large brass bar festooned with vintage shakers.

Named after the famous drink (a Gibson is extremely similar to a Martini), three versions of the Gibson are available at the bar, in addition to an impressive original cocktail menu with 48 drinks from which to choose—yes, 48—with many featuring homemade ingredients and intriguing infusions.

However, despite the variety of Gibsons and extensive menu, make sure you try one of the bar's signature drinks: the Electric Earl. This delicious concoction features an electric daisy, an edible flower that will zap your tongue with a gentle shock at every sip.

MERCHANT HOUSE

13 Well Ct, London, EC4M 9DM
Nearest Tube stop: Mansion House, Bank

It might be tough to find, but it's worth the hunt. Merchant House is one of the most impressive bars dedicated to spirits in London, if not the UK. Decorated with old maps and leather armchairs, the bar features drinks that owe their origins and/or global spread to Britain's imperial history: there are more than 600 whiskies, 400 rums, and 400 gins on offer, as well as Cuban cigars. Obviously, it's impossible to work your way through all of these (at least in one sitting). Luckily, the bar does offer a variety of tasting classes that feature some rare tipples.

The cocktail menu is also special—the bar only offers bespoke serves. Guests choose their favored spirit, one of 15 different flavor profiles, and a subsequent cocktail style (for example, a Gin and Tonic, a Flip, or a Hurricane).

Then there's The Brig. Within the Merchant House space you will discover London's smallest official bar, only available via advance reservation. With a maximum capacity of four people, it's booked by the hour, with all drinks included in the rental price, along with a private bartender.

DINGLE BLACKCURRANT PICKING

An odd hybrid of a Bramble and a Highball, the result is really lovely and refreshing. This recipe was originally conceived to celebrate World Whisky Day.

2 oz. Dingle Distillery Single Pot Still Whiskey

⅓ oz. amaro

⅓ oz. blackcurrant cordial

⅔ oz. soda

Edible flower, to garnish

1. Build all the ingredients carefully in an ice-filled tumbler.
2. Garnish with an edible flower and serve immediately.

BLACK ROCK

9 Christopher St, London, EC2A 2BS
Nearest Tube stop: Liverpool Street/Old Street

The most impressive thing about Black Rock isn't the majestic central table made from a 190-year-old oak tree trunk sawn in half and filling most of the floor space. Rather, it is the 300-bottle whisky collection, proudly displayed in large glass cabinets that punters can happily peruse to their hearts' delight. The whisky is sorted into flavor categories and color-coded by price, making it immediately understandable to newbie and expert alike.

While it's fair to call this space a "bar," there is no actual bar. The staff instead circulates table to table, offering advice and conversation about the whiskies gracing the cabinets. Reflecting that industry's drive toward cocktails, two varieties of Old-Fashioned appear on the menu as well as a number of other classics with a whisky twist. I recommend the Bulleit Rye-based Piña Colada, listed on the menu as a Creole Colada.

Black Rock also offers whisky-blending classes, with a bonus: you can take your one-of-a-kind bottle home with you, created by your own hands, nose, and palate.

MAYOR OF SCAREDY CAT TOWN

12-16 Artillery Ln, London, E1 7LS
Nearest Tube stop: Liverpool Street

To get into the Mayor of Scaredy Cat Town, you first must pass through The Breakfast Club café and restaurant in Spitalfields. At the counter, ask to see the Mayor. A secret refrigerator door entrance will then be opened for you. Don't be a scaredy cat: pass through the portal and enter this excellent basement bar.

When the owners set up shop 11 years ago, London was enjoying a boom in speakeasy venues and the fridge door gimmick led to attention and success. Since then, bar manager Alex Frattini has ensured that standards stay high: "The initial attraction to our bar is most likely our SMEG fridge door entrance and password. However, I have always said to staff and guests that what makes us truly stand out is the excellent hospitality we provide, great drinks, and friendly and knowledgeable staff in a cool and unique environment."

The bar combines retro décor and absurdist art, but most importantly serves stellar drinks. Some examples include Through the Grapevine, which combines many grape-based ingredients, including grappa, vermouth, and Riesling cordial, and the Pick-Me-Up.

You can't ask for more from a refrigerator.

PICK-ME-UP

This indulgent and rich drink, featuring excellent calvados alongside a blend of rich dry sherries, is more likely to knock you out than pick you up.

1 ½ oz. Château du Breuil 8yr Calvados

½ oz. Amaro Montenegro

½ oz. Pedro Ximénez

⅓ oz. oloroso

Lemon zest, to garnish

1. Add all the ingredients to a mixing glass filled with ice and stir until chilled and diluted.
2. Strain over an ice block into a Nick and Nora glass and garnish with lemon zest.

DISCOUNT SUIT COMPANY

29A Wentworth St, London, E1 7TB
Nearest Tube stop: Aldgate East

While there are many hidden speakeasy-style bars throughout London, the Discount Suit Company is one of the originals and best. Though "D SCOUNT SUIT CO PANY" (DSC) is misspelled in enormous rundown letters on the side of its host building, you need to know in advance that the otherwise unmarked bar is found beneath a men's suit store. To enter, push past the thick black curtain at the bottom of the steep staircase.

Located in the former stockroom of a tailor's shop, the DSC was founded in 2014 by experienced hospitality entrepreneur Andy Kerr and quickly gained plaudits for its unbelievably delicious cocktails. Leather chairs and exposed wooden beams bring both rustic charm and a touch of class, while a mannequin in the corner hints at the venue's past. The playlist here is superb, too, with its mix of rock 'n' roll and Northern Soul that gets things swinging.

The DSC serves a rotating list of cocktails based on the classics, and you are highly encouraged to go for something specially made. The cocktail menu hints at other creations while withholding details.

PIÑA FUMADA

Created during the Discount Suit Company's first year in business, it is still on the menu today. This is DSC director Andy Kerr's take on a Mexican favorite. Feel free to experiment with different sodas.

1 ¼ oz. Quiquiriqui Mezcal

¾ oz. fresh lemon juice

¾ oz. pineapple juice

2 teaspoons Velvet Falernum

½ oz. acacia honey

Club soda, to top

Crushed ice, pineapple leaf and lemon wedge, to garnish

1. Add all of the ingredients, except the club soda, to a cocktail shaker filled with ice, shake vigorously until chilled, and strain into a highball glass filled with ice.

2. Top with the club soda and garnish with the crushed ice, pineapple leaf, and lemon wedge.

MILROY'S OF SPITALFIELDS

76 Commercial St, London, E1 6LY
Nearest Tube stop: Aldgate East

Like its Soho counterpart (page 42), Milroy's of Spitalfields features a whisky bar on the ground floor and a basement cocktail bar downstairs. However, this whisky bar is probably England's largest, with more than 1,200 drams on offer. A special members bar one floor up features rare whiskies that you may not find on the ground floor. Though the overall vibe is a little less intimate than Soho, it more than makes up in the superb whisky selection and classy décor.

Owner Martyn "Simo" Simpson wanted to be ambitious when he dreamed up the second Milroy's venue: "Here, we've taken our passion for whisky and curated a collection that takes things to the next level. We've tasted all of it. If we didn't like it, it didn't go on the shelf."

As you can imagine, there's a lot of shelf space for the bar's impressive collection, with many rows of caged bottles running around the walls.

If you're not in the mood for whisky, The Proofing Room cocktail bar occupies the basement of the impressive facility. The focus here is on Highballs, though there's a rotating cocktail menu and bartenders here are happy to invent something to complement your mood and palate.

COCONUT BUTTER OLD-FASHIONED

A classic has now become extra creamy and indulgent.

2 oz. Coconut Butter-infused Buffalo Trace (see recipe)

2 dashes Peychaud's Bitters

2 dashes Angostura Bitters

⅓ oz. simple syrup

1. Add all of the ingredients to a mixing glass with ice, stir, and strain into a chilled rocks glass over ice.

Coconut Butter-infused Buffalo Trace: Heat 2 ¾ oz. coconut butter until it becomes a liquid, and pour into a container along with a full bottle of Buffalo Trace bourbon. Let stand at room temperature for 4 hours before freezing overnight. Remove the coconut butter layer, which can be further filtered by pouring it through a coffee filter. Strain and store.

CENTRAL LONDON

Central London easily contains the highest concentration of bars in the city—and there's a lot of them. They are a reflection of the city center, vying for the attention of the millions of visiting tourists but also the locals who try to avoid said tourists at all costs.

Flashy, expensive establishments sit alongside seedy secret speakeasies and cultures spanning the globe are represented here, all a short walk away from the iconic Trafalgar Square and Westminster, the seat of power of the United Kingdom.

Central London

A. **Pantechnicon**
   19 Motcomb St

B. **FAM Bar & Kitchen**
   Corner of Picton Pl &
   31 Duke St

C. **Bandra Bhai**
   79-81 Mortimer St

D. **Cahoots**
   13 Kingly Ct

E. **Swift**
   12 Old Compton St

F. **Milroy's of SOHO**
   3 Greek St

G. **Café Pacifico**
   5 Langley St

H. **Cellar Door**
   Wellington St

I. **Upstairs at Rules**
   34-35 Maiden Ln

J. **Tattershall Castle**
   Victoria Embankment

K. **Black Parrot**
   8 Bride Ct

PANTECHNICON

19 Motcomb St, London SW1X 8LB
Nearest Tube stop: Knightsbridge

In an impressively renovated 1830s building in the center of Belgravia you'll find the Pantechnicon, where well-to-do locals once stored their excess belongings. Today, after walking past the towering pillars, choose among five floors dedicated to shopping, food, and drink, all inspired by Nordic and Japanese sensibilities. If you find this a strange combination, try it to become a believer.

On the ground floor, Café Kitsune recreates the Parisian coffee experience at its best. The second floor hosts Nordic restaurant Eldr, celebrating "seasonality, sustainability and traditional techniques."

However, on the third floor the all-season roof garden serves beer, cocktails, and produce-led food. Sit outside amongst the greenery, or shelter under the greenhouse during the winter months, and sip on cocktails inspired by Nordic ingredients and elegant simplicity. Try a variety of recommended gin and acquavit offerings, or give their take on a Lingonberry Cosmopolitan a go.

SALTED LEMON GIN FIZZ

This little number has been created by Pantechnicon head mixologist Gento Torigata, designed to be easy to make at home and also impress pals at the same time.

1 ½ oz. gin

½ oz. Salted Honey Lemon liquid

1 wedge Salted Honey Lemon (see recipe), to garnish

Soda water, to top

1. Stir the gin and Salted Honey Lemon Liquid together before pouring into a highball glass with ice.

2. Top with soda water and garnish with the salted honey lemon wedge.

Salted Honey Lemon: In a small container, combine 7 oz. honey, 3 ½ oz. water, and ⅓ oz. table salt and mix well. Slice a lemon into 8 wedges, place the wedges in the container with the honey mixture, and soak overnight, covered, before using.

FAM BAR & KITCHEN

Corner of Picton Pl & 31 Duke St,
London, W1U 1LG
Nearest Tube stop: Bond Street

FAM Bar provides a moment of peace in the atmosphere of a neighborhood bar surrounded by bustling central London. The cocktails are top drawer and competitively priced. The bar features an all-star team of mixologists at its helm, including Dre Masso, a leading figure in London's cocktail scene for the past two decades.

Only a stone's throw away from Oxford Street, you'll not have to walk far after a shopping spree to enjoy one of FAM's unique creations, and their mixologists champion local producers. Don't forget to try the house Margarita that the bar is rightfully proud of. It features a custom blend of three tequilas. The soundtrack to your evening will come from one of the various vinyl records stacked and waiting their turn to be spun.

This is a cocktail bar without pretention. Pop in on a whim, without worrying about dressing for the occasion. You'll find an intimate atmosphere inside, with seating for only 50 and a few more on the outside terrace.

FAM MARGARITA

The secret behind FAM Bar's famous Margaritas is the special tequila blend it uses to make the drink. A dash of sweet honey water doesn't hurt either.

1 ¾ oz. tequila blend (Olmeca Altos Plata, Tequila Ocho Plata, Fortaleza Reposado)

¾ oz. fresh lemon juice

⅞ oz. Devon Flower Honey Water (1 part wildflower honey to 1 part water, stirred together)

Lemon thyme sprig, to garnish

1. Add all of the ingredients to a cocktail shaker filled with ice, shake vigorously until chilled, and double-strain over ice into a rocks glass.
2. Garnish with the lemon thyme sprig.

BANDRA BHAI

79-81 Mortimer St, London W1W 7SJ
Nearest Tube stop: Oxford Circus

A secret "smuggler's den" is hidden beneath the streets of Fitzrovia that will transport you in time and place to 1970s India. You'll find no sign at street level. To get there, weave your way through the ground level of the Pali Hill restaurant and descend a set of stairs to the door concealed in a concrete wall. Manage the arrival and you will be rewarded with one of London's oddest bars.

While "kitsch" and "gawdy"—their words, not mine—might not be adjectives sought by London's more upmarket establishments (especially around Oxford Circus), Bandra Bhai is unashamedly both, and succeeds wonderfully in evoking Bollywood's psychedelic Golden Age, with trinkets in every corner, velvet upholstery, and animal print rugs.

The cocktails themselves are expertly crafted by head barman Dav Eames, who has delivered Indian-themed twists on old classics. Try their Spicy Jaggery Old-Fashioned, made with unrefined sugar, chat masala, and aromatic bitters.

CAHOOTS

13 Kingly Ct, Carnaby, London W1B 5PW
Nearest Tube stop: Oxford Circus

Since opening in 2015, Cahoots has quickly become one of the better-known themed bars in London, taking its clientele back to 1940s post-war jubilance. As you descend the wooden escalator to the underground bunker prepare to sip cocktails in a reworked subway carriage.

You might be in time to hear a wartime sing-along around the bar's piano. Or join in on the swing dancing that occurs on a nightly basis. There are actually three spaces within Cahoots: the Underground and the Control Room are both found downstairs while the Ticket Hall is on the ground floor. In each room, the clock has been turned back to 1946, as seen in every detail from carpets to lampshades, while each space has its own distinctive cocktails. Make the time to visit all three.

Cahoots packages many of its cocktails into "ration cocktail bags," delivered and designed to make at home—but experiencing the unique surroundings will bring them to life.

KEEP MARM AND CARRY ON

This is a more accessible version of Cahoots's twist on a Pornstar Martini and has been on the drinks menu ever since the bar opened.

1 ¼ oz. vodka (Cahoots uses Smirnoff Black)

½ oz. fresh lemon juice

1 ½ oz. passion fruit juice (can be substituted with a mix of ¾ oz. orange juice and ¾ oz. pineapple juice)

2 teaspoons simple syrup

Digestive biscuit, to garnish

1 tablespoon lemon curd (or marmalade), to garnish

1. Add all of the ingredients to an ice-filled shaker and shake vigorously for 10 seconds. If using a jug, stir for 30 seconds.
2. Strain into a teacup over a couple of ice cubes, alongside the digestive biscuit topped with the lemon curd.

SWIFT

12 Old Compton St, London, W1D 4TQ
Nearest Tube stop: Tottenham Court Road/Covent
Garden/Leicester Square

Located in central Soho, Swift is one of London's (and the world's) most acclaimed bars, a regular on the widely respected list of World's 50 Best Bars. The pet project of Bobby Hiddleston and Mia Johanssen, the couple first cut their teeth at some of the world's other top bars, including Milk and Honey, Dead Rabbit, and Calooh Callay (Page 62).

The bar is divided into two areas. The more casual ground floor features refreshing drinks and classic cocktails. The Irish Coffee here is renowned, and a perfect pick-me-up before or after a West End theater show.

The more serious action is below, in the basement—and requires a reservation so you won't be disappointed. This space goes for something a little more decadent, with table service, art deco leather furniture, mirrored walls, and a cocktail list favoring darker spirits. To add to the mood, there's live jazz every weekend. It's also a phenomenal place to savor a whisky, with a selection of more than 300 drams.

SWIFT IRISH COFFEE

"We are most famous for our Irish Coffee," says co-founder Bobby Hiddleston. "It doesn't have any unusual ingredients; instead we worked on perfecting each simple step. We keep the coffee and glasses in a sous vide to maintain the perfect service temperature, we created our own coffee blend with an independent roaster to suit our flavor balance, and we buy and prepare the best quality local cream."

Even if you don't manage to be as exact as Hiddleston in your preparation, this should still be very delicious and perk you right up.

2 ½ oz. demerara-sweetened filter coffee

1 ½ oz. Jameson Stout Edition

Whipped chilled double cream

Freshly grated nutmeg, to garnish

1. Pour the sweetened coffee into a warm mug or other heat-resistant glass, stirring well to make sure all of the sugar is dissolved.

2. Add the Irish whiskey and stir again.

3. Float the cream on top by pouring it over the back of a spoon.

4. Garnish with the grated nutmeg.

MILROY'S OF SOHO

3 Greek St, London, W1D 4NX
Nearest Tube stop: Tottenham Court Road

Milroy's is an institution for the whisky industry and hardcore whisky fans alike. The original Milroy's was founded by brothers Jack and Wallace, who in 1964 were among the first vendors to make single malt whisky trendy. Eventually, they sold the company and bar, and the establishment slowly suffered under subsequent owners.

Current owner Martyn "Simo" Simpson then took over in 2014 and has put Milroy's back on the map as a venue for all lovers of whisky, as well as for industry figures to meet and catch up. The bar is small and intimate and houses 500 top-quality whiskies as well as a fully operational whisky shop and tiny tasting room that struggles to fit more than five or six people at a time.

Milroy's has a secret, however. At the back of the bar a bookcase opens to reveal a staircase down to The Vaults, a basement speakeasy. Lit by candles with a décor of exposed brick walls and handmade tables, the venue regularly hosts live jazz in addition to serving superb drinks. However, the best spot in the bar is the tiny room at the back, shaped and paneled like the inside of a whisky cask.

LONDON TO KENTUCKY

While the whiskeys featured in this cocktail are superb, the walnut wine, fig liqueur, and bitters will help wrestle with their woody profiles.

1 ½ oz. Wild Turkey 101 Bourbon

⅓ oz. green walnut wine

⅓ oz. fig liqueur

1 teaspoon Russell's Reserve 6-Year-Old Rye

2 dashes Angostura Bitters

Orange twist, to garnish

1. Build in a rocks glass and stir well with a large ice cube.
2. Garnish with the orange twist.

CAFÉ PACIFICO

5 Langley St, London, WC2H 9JA
Nearest Tube stop: Covent Garden

Founded in 1982 and still going strong, Café Pacifico was London's first serious Mexican restaurant and evolved into an institution as the city and neighborhood changed radically around it over the decades.

The restaurant itself, styled as a Mexican cantina, is a riot of color. The painted tiles, chairs, framed photos, and expansive murals wouldn't be out of place in Latin America. And while the standard of the food has remained high, the drinks are why you go there. Café Pacifico's legendary, award-winning margaritas should be mandatory for any visit, and there's a wide variety from which to choose, including the Fruit Margarita, which lines the glass with both salt and chili. Most of the cocktails on offer feature tequila or rum, while other options, such as a Caipirinha or a Pisco Sour, also fit the Latin theme.

Then there's the selection of agaves. There are hundreds of tequilas and mezcals proudly displayed at the bar; a good way to start tackling them is to go for one of the available flight options that provides a variety to try at cheap prices (at least by London standards).

CELLAR DOOR

Wellington St, London, WC2R 0HS
Nearest Tube stop: Temple/Covent Garden

Don't let the tacky decorations and messy, dated website fool you; Cellar Door is a top cabaret bar serving excellent cocktails—a cozy secret basement surprise in the heart of London.

Live entertainment is a constant feature. Drag shows, burlesque nights, drag-queen bingo, live music, and more are all on the program. The cocktail menu is extensive, featuring classics, historical cocktails, and the bar team's own creations. Also, if you ask at the bar, you can buy something that you can snort: snuff! A wide variety of flavors is available.

The bar itself is a converted Victorian public men's toilet that had achieved some notoriety back in the day: Oscar Wilde was arrested there before being sent to Reading prison. Speaking of toilets, Cellar Door has some of the most unusual you'll find. The stalls are made of see-through glass and frost over only when the door is locked.

UPSTAIRS AT RULES

34-35 Maiden Ln, London, WC2E 7LB
Nearest Tube stop: Charing Cross/Covent Garden

Britain's oldest restaurant, founded in 1798 and still going, is one of the city's gastronomic institutions. While its upstairs cocktail bar isn't as old, there's no doubting its quality. Formerly the private dining room where King Edward VII courted actress Lillie Langtry, the bar radiates old-school, upper-class English elegance—imagine the kind of place where Winston Churchill might have wanted to smoke a cigar. If this sounds too stuffy, the recent addition of the Winter Terrace adds a new and more open atrium space filled with plants and artwork.

As for the drinks, the menu was created by Brian Silva, an American and one of London's longest-serving master bartenders (he has set up and led countless bars in the city over decades). While he emphasizes perfect execution of the classics, the menu also features his original creations, such as the Rules Royale, showcasing Chartreuse and violet liqueur, or the Naughty Mac, made with sherry-matured Scotch and hellfire bitters.

Upstairs at Rules also boasts a truly special cocktail masterclass—on Tuesday and Thursday afternoons, Silva will teach you how to make a number of classic cocktails as well as some of your own choosing.

TATTERSHALL CASTLE

Victoria Embankment, London, SW1A 2HR
Nearest Tube stop: Embankment

In a previous life, the Tattershall Castle—despite the name, a ship—served 40 years as a passenger ferry operating across the Humber River before being retired in 1973. After a stint as a floating art gallery, it opened up shop a stone's throw from Westminster in 1982.

Now known as "The Pub on the Thames," it operates as just that, as well as a restaurant and party venue. It hosts live music and comedy nights, and can be booked for private soirées. After 11 p.m., the venue "closes" and converts into a nightclub.

A party boat is already fun, but its berth across from the London Eye and the Waterloo waterfront make it still more special. On a good day with clear skies (this is London, after all), the view at sunset is hard to beat. However, it's not recommended for those prone to sea-sickness as the boat does rock ever so slightly.

BLACK PARROT

8 Bride Ct, London, EC4Y 8DU
Nearest Tube stop: Blackfriars

Fleet Street was once famous as the headquarters of many British media organizations and publishers—so much so that "Fleet Street" is often used as short-hand for the entire British press establishment (even though most have relocated elsewhere). Tucked away off a little alleyway is where you'll find the Black Parrot.

Formerly the Fleet Street branch of Merchant House (page 18), the bar was recently rebranded as Black Parrot and now specializes almost exclusively in rum. With more than 300 different bottles, it's one of the most extensive bar collections in the UK, if not Europe. Naturally, all the cocktails here are rum based, including the Old-Fashioned.

Though an impressive houseplant collection may suggest a Caribbean rainforest, plush velvet seats, low lighting, and plenty of games, including an 18-foot shuffleboard, betray the real goal of the bar: providing a space for people to relax and put their troubles aside for a little while.

The bar also offers rum masterclasses on Saturdays that include a welcome cocktail and four different rums from the Black Parrot's extensive collection, featuring a rare offering that may be tricky to find anywhere else.

EAST LONDON

Historically, East London was the seedy part of the city, which also received many waves of immigrants from around the world over centuries. But, starting in the 1990s, it established itself as London's main creative hub. Though the areas of Shoreditch and Brick Lane get a lot of attention, there is a vibrant community of independent businesses throughout this part of the city, including music venues and restaurants, and some of the world's best graffiti and street art can be found here as well.

It figures that this neighborhood is also home to some of the city's best bars.

East London

A. Three Sheets
510b Kingsland Rd

B. Hacha
378 Kingsland Rd

C. Calooh Callay
65 Rivington Rd

D. Seed Library
100 Shoreditch High St

E. The Last Tuesday Society
11 Mare St

F. Coupette
423 Bethnal Green Rd

G. The Sun Tavern
441 Bethnal Green Rd

H. Satan's Whiskers
343 Cambridge Heath Rd

I. Alfred Le Roy
Queen's Yard, White Post Ln

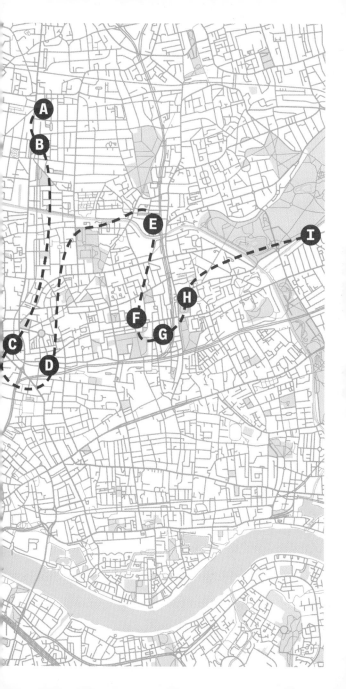

THREE SHEETS

510b Kingsland Rd, London, E8 4AB
Nearest Tube stop: Dalston Junction (Overground)

Renowned in Dalston, Three Sheets at first glance seems to be a very unassuming boxy little venue. A casual patron certainly wouldn't clock that this is actually an award-winning cocktail bar, considered one of the UK's best. Founded by brothers Noel and Max Venning from Manchester, the bar specializes in minimalist cocktails that pack a powerfully complex punch at night. Demurely, during the day they serve coffee.

Look carefully and the décor matches the approach to drinks—it's a cozy and tasteful space. An exposed brick wall overlooks marble tables. Leather stools are propped up against the bar. The constantly rotating menu tends to feature creative takes on classics. The Earth Martini, for example, highlights beetroot and olive oil. Little wonder that this tiny venue is often full of people.

FORAGED MARTINI

A perfect example of Three Sheets's minimalist approach, a typical Martini is given a slightly sweet and herbal dimension, transforming it into a different kind of drink altogether.

1 ¾ oz. London Dry gin

2 teaspoons dry vermouth

1 teaspoons nettle cordial

Sprig of baby's breath, to garnish

1. Combine all of the ingredients in a mixing glass with ice and stir to dilute and chill.

2. Double strain into a coupette and garnish with the baby's breath sprig.

HACHA

378 Kingsland Rd, London, E8 4AA
Nearest Tube stop: Haggerston (Overground)

The agave craze that has swept the States hasn't quite made its way over to the UK and Europe yet. But there are a few missionaries doing their best to convert the heathen masses. Hacha cofounders Emma Murphy and Deano Moncrieffe—the latter a brand ambassador for Don Julio tequila—are spreading the good word through their excellent agave-oriented bar.

Unlike other specialized spirits joints that often feature an encyclopedic selection, Hacha has only 25 spirits—a selection of tequila, mezcal, soto, and raicilla—available behind the bar. That said, the choices here are rotated constantly, and that means every visit to Hacha is a chance to try something new while surrounded by cacti and other succulents. Moncrieffe fervently believes that less is more, and the limited selection encourages customers to be adventurous. A few different flight options allow you to taste your way through the carefully-curated menu.

The drinks themselves are complemented by kitchen partners Maiz Azul cooking up a Mexican storm. There is a healthy selection of agave-based cocktails—Hacha's menu spotlights the Mirror Margarita which, despite its varied ingredients, including grapefruit zest and a custom sour mix, manages to remain completely transparent.

PINK NEGRONI

A very boozy summery serve that is also dangerously quaffable. The herbal notes of the tequila and eucalyptus are balanced out by peaches and floral tones from the infused Cocchi.

⅞ oz. Patrón Silver Tequila

⅔ oz. Rinquinquin

1 oz. Rosehip Cocchi (see recipe)

5 dashes Eucalyptus Tincture (see recipe)

Eucalyptus leaf, to garnish

1. Add all of the ingredients to a mixing glass, stir, and pour into a rocks glass over ice.

2. Garnish with the eucalyptus leaf.

Rosehip Cocchi: Add 4 rosehip teabags to 1 bottle of Cocchi Rosa and let steep for 1 hour.

Eucalyptus Tincture: Add 15–20 eucalyptus leaves to 100 ml of vodka and let steep for 24 hours before straining and storing.

CALOOH CALLAY

65 Rivington St, London, EC2A 3AY
Nearest Tube stop: Shoreditch High St
(Overground)

Shoreditch, one of London's main entertainment hubs in the nineteenth and early twentieth centuries before becoming a working-class neighborhood, is now a thriving center for all things hip and fashionable. Independent shops, cafes, and bars are everywhere. Some of the world's best graffiti and street art can be found here, too.

At the heart of Shoreditch's bar scene beats Calooh Callay. One of the area's first cocktail bars when it opened in 2008, it consistently rakes in awards and praise from the cognoscenti. Named after a nonsense phrase in Lewis Carroll's famous poem, "The Jabberwocky," to Emily Chipperfield, its head of bars, the moniker represents something more substantial: "It's a poem written by a serious author and mathematician yet with made-up words. This leads to our ethos of 'serious nonsense': We take our craft seriously but don't take ourselves seriously."

An understated entrance reveals a quirky riot within. Honoring its Shoreditch setting, art and graffiti made by local artists is featured throughout the bar, complementing dark walls, a mishmash of furnishings, and a cabaret vibe. The cocktail menu rotates regularly, so there's always a reason to come back.

Let's not forget the secret bar as well. Ask the bartender nicely and she or he might let you into The JubJub. A wardrobe entrance reveals a secret staircase that leads to a special tiny bar area adorned with neon lights.

RED FLAGS

Where Highballs are usually very fresh, this one has loads of added depth thanks to the fruity and dry flavors provided by the vermouth and sherry. A little added salt helps balance things out.

1 oz. Spearhead Scotch whisky

2 teaspoons Tio Pepe Fino Sherry

¾ oz. Regal Rogue Bold Red Vermouth

1 teaspoon sugar syrup

2 dashes orange bitters

Pinch of salt

Top up with Franklin & Sons Light Tonic

Orange twist, to garnish

1. Build your drink in a highball glass.

2. Fill with ice and garnish with the orange twist.

SEED LIBRARY

100 Shoreditch High St, London, E1 6HU
Nearest Tube stop: Shoreditch High Street
(Overground)

The latest creation of bar entrepreneur Ryan Cheti-yawardana, Seed Library is a celebration of innova-tive minimalism in the beating heart of London's hipster culture. Located in the basement of the One Hundred Shoreditch hotel, it looks like a cozy lounge bar where cartoon villains might want to relax—stone walls, low light, mushroom-shaped resin lamps, plush orange-and-dark-red seats.

A different proposition to Lyaness (page 104), Che-tiyawardana gently twists simple, classic cocktail, enhanced by analogous flavors sourced from unusual ingredients: "We want to look at our bias; the approach, ingredients, knowledge, and where we source from within the industry and to step away from this, leaving more of a 'hands-off' reflection of the final product."

As examples, the Coriander Seed Gimlet uses coriander cordial to add an herbal tang to the classic drink. The Galangal Penicillin (featured at right) combines tequila and mezcal for herbal smoky notes, while galangal hon-ey replaces the ginger traditionally used in the drink.

As with Lyaness, Chetiyawardana seeks to highlight specific ingredients. But in this case, the goal is to serve a classic cocktail's flavor profile rather than build a drink from scratch: "Working with different producers and suppliers, we're letting their products fulfill these central roles in our cocktails, but doing very little to over-polish them, allowing all their fuzziness and idiosyncrasies to shine through."

GALANGAL PENICILLIN

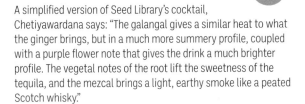

A simplified version of Seed Library's cocktail, Chetiyawardana says: "The galangal gives a similar heat to what the ginger brings, but in a much more summery profile, coupled with a purple flower note that gives the drink a much brighter profile. The vegetal notes of the root lift the sweetness of the tequila, and the mezcal brings a light, earthy smoke like a peated Scotch whisky."

1 ½ oz. blanco tequila

2 teaspoons Aperol

1 teaspoon mezcal

½ oz. fresh lime juice

⅔ oz. galangal honey

Edible flower, to garnish

1. Combine all of the ingredients in a cocktail shaker with ice, shake, and strain into a rocks glass over ice.

2. Garnish with an edible flower of your choice.

THE LAST TUESDAY SOCIETY

Victoria Buildings, 11 Mare St, London, E8 4RP
Nearest Tube stop: Cambridge Heath (Overground)

The Last Tuesday Society is not a bar at all but rather, as the name suggests, a society. Founded in 1873 at Harvard University by philosopher William James, it is dedicated to the unusual, interesting, and surreal, and has been hosting events and lectures throughout its history.

The society migrated to London in physical form in 2008, taking up residence at its current address, evolving into what it describes as "a sort of hybrid between a shop and a museum, an academic institution and an art gallery, an installation and a performance."

The result of a successful crowdfunding campaign saw the addition of one of the most unusual cocktail bars in London, opening on Halloween, 2014. Although officially part of the Last Tuesday Society, the bar itself is known as The Absinthe Parlour. Voted the best bar in London at the seventh annual Design My Night Awards in 2019, its absinthe menu was also shortlisted for Imbibe's Specialist List of the Year.

Crammed with curiosities, every space of the bar is filled with the unusual and macabre. Sip a cocktail while staring down a turtle skeleton suspended from the ceiling!

COUPETTE

423 Bethnal Green Rd, London, E2 0AN
Nearest Tube stop: Bethnal Green

Founded by former Beaufort Bar head bartender Chris Moore, Coupette has established itself as one of the hospitality industry's favorite hangouts with an unpretentious and sleek vibe as well as outstanding drinks.

This award-winning bar aims to bring a little bit of France to London, a decision that was mostly commercial, according to bar manager Andrei Marcu: "There was a gap in the market. There are many French fine dining or French restaurants in London but not many cocktail bars that are French-inspired. And there is so much to work with in the drinks side of the French culture. It just made sense."

Coupette specializes in creating deceptively simple serves that also require extensive background preparation, often using French spirits: calvados, cognac, Champagne, vin jaune, and all kinds of French liqueurs and bitters.

However, anyone who knows Coupette will recommend starting the drinking experience there with the same two drinks before exploring the rest of the menu. The now-famous cocktail named Apples is a shifting study in apple flavors as the calvados and carbonated apple juice used changes every month. The Champagne Piña Colada combines rhum agricole, coconut sorbet, and, of course, Champagne, to form a gloriously indulgent concoction.

BOARD ROOM

One of Coupette's classic drinks, this cocktail is meant
to evoke board rooms of the past with cigar smoke in the air, rich
Cognacs, red wines, and coffee being drunk, and fancy walnut
paneling and furniture.

1 ½ oz. Hennessy Fine
¾ oz. Dubonnet
2 teaspoons Cherry Heering
¼ oz. Noix de la Saint Jean Liqueur
¼ oz. simple syrup
½ teaspoon Mr Black Coffee Liqueur
2 dashes walnut bitters

1. Add all of the ingredients to a mixing glass, add ice, and stir.

2. Strain into a rocks glass over 2 large ice spheres.

3. Optional extra step: use a smoke gun to smoke the rocks glass
   with cherrywood before pouring the drink in. Vive la France.

THE SUN TAVERN

441 Bethnal Green Rd, London, E2 0AN
Nearest Tube stop: Bethnal Green

Another Andy Kerr project and sister bar to the Discount Suit Company (page 24), The Sun Tavern looks like a typical pub on the outside but actually is a world-class booze establishment—especially when it comes to Irish whiskey and poitín.

More than 200 bottles of Irish whiskey weigh the shelves, but the bar is proudest of its collection of poitín (pronounced poh-cheen), an Irish spirit usually made from grains in a pot still. Eager to evangelize, The Sun Tavern hosts poitín masterclasses and masterminded the annual World Poitín Day celebration that occurs every November.

Other drinks aren't neglected, however. The bar keeps ten local beers on tap—regularly rotated—and the house lager and pale ale are produced exclusively for it by the Portobello Road Brewery.

The cocktails also happen to be irresistible. Looking for something contemporary? Try the Highball, F*ck Vladimir Poitín, which blends the named spirit with peated Irish whiskey in addition to soda and floral tea syrup, or the drink simply named The Punch, which serves four and is arguably the best choice to kick off a night of partying.

TWO IRISH MEN

A longtime staple at The Sun Tavern, this whiskey-based Manahattan variation is surprisingly soft if the right Irish whiskey is used.

1 ¼ oz. Irish whiskey

⅞ oz. Cocchi Americano

2 teaspoons Bénédictine

1 dash Peychaud's Bitters

Lemon twist, to garnish

1. Fill a mixing glass with ice, add all of the ingredients, and stir until chilled.

2. Strain into a coupette and garnish with a lemon twist.

SATAN'S WHISKERS

343 Cambridge Heath Rd, London E2 9RA
Nearest Tube stop: Bethnal Green

Bethnal Green's neighborhood cocktail bar offers a changing daily menu, meaning that even next-door residents always have a reason to return. Although it's hard to predict what's happening on any given night, it's reasonable to expect unusual twists on old classics. Opening in 2013, it can't have been easy to establish a well-regarded drinking joint in an area bursting with excellent options. Yet, Satan's Whiskers has managed to earn a spot as one of the best cocktail bars in London.

Equally known for its soundtrack and its cocktails, fans of hip-hop are well catered to, with a playlist impeccably curated from open to close.

Satan's Whiskers makes the most of its combination of cocktails, music, and décor: Taxidermy emerges from exposed bricks, giving the soundtrack a surreal setting to enjoy unique and ever-changing cocktails. Pre-batched cocktails are also available for takeout.

A food menu is also available, consisting of bar snacks and vegetarian options, as well as suggested themed cocktail pairings.

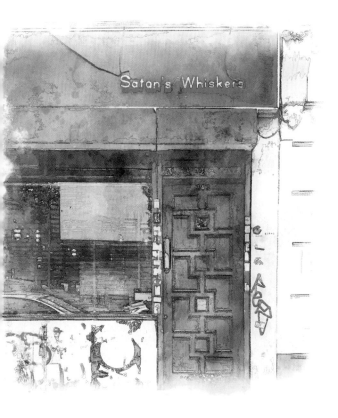

ALFRED LE ROY

CRATE Brewery, Queen's Yard, White Post Ln,
Mooring E9 5EN
Nearest Tube stop: Hackney Wick (Overground)

The area of Hackney Wick has been experiencing a vibrant revival over the last decade. Thanks to low rental rates on studios, all kinds of artists and creative types have moved into this previously rundown neighborhood and turned it into an exciting area to explore.

Here is where you'll also find the CRATE Brewery. Not only does it make beer, pizza, and host the world's first zero-waste restaurant, it has also converted a dilapidated canal boat into a delightful and intimate cocktail bar. The passion project of Ben Perkins, he collaborated with the CRATE team to make a former pleasure cruiser ship-shape again. Docked beside the brewery, Alfred Le Roy offers a hip, boozy floating maritime alternative to Tattershall Castle (page 50). The owners kept the boat's original name in honor of the landlord of a well-known Belgian pub.

Alfred can be hired out for boozy cruises down the River Lea.

NORTH LONDON

On the whole, North London is a little calmer than most other parts of the city. There are exceptions of course, such as the tourist-heavy areas of Camden or bustling Islington. As a result, it is derided and admired in equal parts for being "bougie"; avoiding the ostentatious displays of wealth typical of West London, the playful chaos of South London, and the gritty and hip vibes of East London in favor of understated class.

The bars here are a reflection of this—with very few exceptions they cater almost exclusively to local residents, and the most successful are deeply valued by their neighbors.

North London

A. Little Bat
54 Islington Park St

B. Laki Kane
144-145 Upper St

C. Homeboy
108 Essex Rd

D. The Gunmakers
13 Eyre St Hill

E. Tayēr + Elementary
152 Old St

F. Happiness Forgets
8-9 Hoxton Square

G. Doña
92 Stoke Newington High St

LITTLE BAT

54 Islington Park St, London, N1 1PX
Nearest Tube stop: Highbury & Islington

A sister bar to Calooh Callay (page 62), Little Bat is a high-quality, low-key neighborhood bar designed—with its globes, books, and tasseled lampshades—as a cross between a library and a quaint museum.

However, the décor matters less than the drinks. The rum punch consists of mostly rum (and a little rum liqueur). Le Ritz is an homage to French spirits, including calvados, cognac, and Moet & Chandon Champagne. Another house specialty, the Big Smoke Gamble (featured here), pits bourbon against peated Scotch from Ardbeg, with a touch of smoked honey to mediate the ensuing battle.

To complement this lineup of cocktails, try the excellent small platters menu, which features mostly Mexican-inspired fare.

The bar also runs tasting events across different spirit categories at phenomenal prices; for example, a recent showcase of calvados brand Sassy cost a mere £10 a ticket.

BIG SMOKE GAMBLE

You could say this is based on an Old-Fashioned, but the added smoke, provided by the honey and the Ardbeg, threatens to upset the old order. The Maker's 46 barely holds things together.

1 ¼ oz. Maker's Mark 46

½ oz. Ardbeg Wee Beastie

⅔ oz. Lapsang Honey (see recipe)

Orange peel, to garnish

1. Build the drink in a rocks glass with ice and stir.
2. Garnish with an orange peel.

Lapsang Honey: Brew some lapsang tea, strain, and mix with an equal amount of honey.

LAKI KANE

144-145 Upper St, London, N1 1QY
Nearest Tube stop: Highbury & Islington

Laki Kane, a shrine to tiki culture, is a five-star tropical-resort bar in north London that unapologetically celebrates its inspirations—Polynesia, Jamaica, Hawaii, and many other sultry locations are represented here. Rope ladders, bongo drum tables, and Polynesian fire dancers on Friday nights are spread between two floors.

The large number of tiki-themed cocktails often use ingredients found south of the equator. In the mood for a party? Try one of the sharing cocktails—the electric blue Tahitian Free Diver needs a minimum of six people ready to drink it, and you'll likely want more friends at the ready to handle a surfboard lit up with sparklers carrying 20 (or even 40) custom tropical shots.

Then there's the rum. A wide selection graces the menu and the bar also hosts rum-tasting sessions and cocktail masterclasses. A workshop teaches you how to make your own spiced rum (while tasting seven other rums in the process) that you can re-order by the bottle in the future.

TROPICOLADA #2

This is an easygoing drink that aside from the little bit of booze in it contains nothing but healthy ingredients. Because of the coconut cream and yogurt it's got a nice thick smoothie-like consistency.

1 ¾ oz. Yaguara Cachaça (or any cachaça)

1 oz. pineapple juice

1 oz. coconut water

1 oz. Re'al Coconut Cream

⅔ oz. Re'al Agave Syrup, or honey

1 teaspoon yogurt

Avocado slice and mint sprig, to garnish

1. Blend all ingredients together without ice and then blend them again with ice.
2. Pour it into a cocktail glass or tiki mug and garnish with the avocado slice and sprig of mint.

HOMEBOY

108 Essex Rd, London, N1 8LX
Nearest Tube stop: Angel

Homeboy's goal is to put a modern face on time-honored traditions of Irish hospitality. The creation of experienced bartenders and co-founders Aaron Wall and Ciarán Smith, Homeboy has already garnered loads of praise for its laid-back approach and top-quality drinks. The hip-hop and R & B playlists are also excellent.

In addition to a strong collection of Irish whiskeys and beers (including draft Guinness done just right), the cocktails are amazing. There's an extensive menu of classics, but also many original creations, such as the Wogan (featured here), or the punchy Blackthorn No. 2, mixing whiskey, port, and absinthe.

Make sure to try one of the Irish Coffee choices, a signal of Homeboy's dedication to the drink. The bar even sells bottles of its own custom coffee bitters so that aficionados can make their own perfect Irish Coffee at home.

Be sure not to miss the chance to peek into Homeboy's tiny "bar in a bar" at the back of the venue—a mirrored door conceals what is billed as "London's smallest Irish pub."

THE WOGAN

Homeboy co-founder Aaron Wall has created a cocktail honoring the great Irish TV personality that, in his words, is dry and elegant like the man himself.

1 ½ oz. Teeling Small Batch Irish Whiskey

2 teaspoons apricot liqueur

½ oz. fresh lime juice

½ oz. simple syrup

Pinch of salt or 3 dashes 20:1 saline solution

1. Combine all of the ingredients in a cocktail shaker with ice, shake well, and strain into a frozen coupe.

THE GUNMAKERS

13 Eyre St Hill, London, EC1R 5ET
Nearest Tube stop: Farringdon

Lovingly described as a "cocktail pub," the Gunmakers is the result of four pals chasing their dream, according to co-owner Allan Gage: "We are old friends who wanted to fulfill a dream of jointly owning a pub. So we bought one!" However, it's also worth noting that this is also another project from the team behind acclaimed cocktail bar Nine Lives (page 108)—so there's plenty of experienced hands in charge of this operation.

Though the exterior may resemble a Victorian-style establishment typical throughout London, this pub now specializes in high-quality agave drinks, although there's a small selection of excellent beers, too. Try A la Antigua, which features peanut butter-washed tequila, or the Margarita Picante if you're feeling adventurous (yes—it's spicy), or a regular Margarita or Paloma if you'd prefer to stick to classics. A healthy mix of high-end tequilas and mezcals are also available neat, as well as a rotating menu of T&Ts (tequila and tonic).

Tigre Tacos holds permanent residence at the bar and whips up excellent tacos as well as sharing platters that include an excellent ceviche.

And yes, there are Taco Tuesdays.

MARGARITA PICANTE

As you can guess by the name, this is one spicy fiesta of a drink.

1 ½ oz. Tequileño Blanco

2 teaspoons raicilla

⅞ oz. Picante Syrup (see recipe)

⅞ oz. fresh lime juice

1. Add all of the ingredients to a cocktail shaker with ice and shake hard.

2. Strain into a rocks glass over fresh cubed ice with a sea-salted rim.

Picante Syrup: Thinly slice 4 jalapeños; set aside. Combine 1 cup water with 1 cup sugar in a saucepan over medium heat and cook until the sugar dissolves, stirring frequently. Add the jalapeños, 1 tablespoon fresh lime juice, and a pinch of salt and remove from heat. Let steep for 10 minutes and then pour the mixture into a blender and puree. Strain and refrigerate to store.

TAYĒR +
ELEMENTARY

152 Old St, London, EC1V 9BW
Nearest Tube stop: Old Street

Already known as two of the world's best bartend-ers, expectations were high for Alex Kratena's and Monica Berg's new project, Tayēr + Elementary, when it opened in 2019. In 2020, it was ranked #5 on the list of the World's 50 Best Bars, rising to #2 the year after. Obviously, the drinks here are superb.

Tayēr + Elementary is split into two spaces. Elementary is a smaller casual venue with a passing resemblance to a Japanese izakaya, featuring excellent pre-batched cocktails served in seconds, own-label wine and beer, and tasty tapas on the side.

Tayēr (meant to evoke the Spanish word *taller*—work-shop) is only open in the evenings, and is a darker, more intimate space dominated by an enormous horse-shoe-shaped bar where the bartenders work their magic. While the cocktail menu rotates regularly, generally the drinks here look simple and classy but disguise the significant advance preparation required for their ingredients. The results are worth it.

HAPPINESS FORGETS

8-9 Hoxton Square, London, N1 6NU
Nearest Tube stop: Old Street

This small basement bar doesn't look like anything special, merely a homey neighborhood joint. Don't be fooled: Happiness Forgets—named after a Dionne Warwick lyric—is considered by London's top hospitality professionals to be one of the best bars in the city, and the world: a regular stop for locals looking to avoid the bustle of Shoreditch and bartenders who want to learn the tricks of the trade. Known for superb drinks and sterling service delivered with relaxed informality and slick professionalism, you won't forget the happiness that makes this the ultimate local bar experience.

As a result, reservations are recommended. Half the bar is actually saved for walk-ins, but these tables are usually full.

Three cocktails have been available since the bar opened in 2012. The Perfect Storm is a variation on a Dark and Stormy, the Tokyo Collins is a refreshing gin cocktail, and the Jerezana is a study in sherry, drawing out creamy citrus notes. The other cocktails, usually 12 of them, are regularly rotated and always delicious.

Now entrenched in the London drinks scene, Happiness Forgets's low-key approach is reflected in its motto: "Great cocktails—no wallies" (translation from British English: "idiots").

THE PERFECT STORM

One of the bar's classic drinks. The plum brandy packs
a surprising punch and adds a lot of depth. Make sure you use
fresh juices to really give the drink a tangy zing or it may fall a
little flat.

1 ½ oz. demerara rum

1 teaspoon La Vieille Prune (plum brandy)

½ oz. honey

½ oz. ginger juice

⅔ oz. fresh lemon juice

1 lemon wedge, to garnish

1. Add all of the ingredients to a cocktail shaker filled with ice and
   shake hard.
2. Strain into a collins glass filled with ice and garnish with a lemon
   wedge.

DOÑA

92 Stoke Newington High St, London, N16 7NY
Nearest Tube Station: Rectory Road

Artfully decorated with Mexican-inspired glamour, pink-and-deep-red upholstery, Doña is part Mexican cantina and part 1920s Harlem jazz club. Though a one-stop shop for all things tequila and mezcal related, the bar also serves as an arts space dedicated mainly to female-fronted events and acts. This is important to co-owners Thea Cumming and Lucia Massey. "As female founders of a late-night space, we are in the minority," says Massey. "The nightlife industry is dominated by men and 'the masculine,' so it was important that the aesthetic overtly championed strong feminine energy. We wanted it to feel sexy but also safe, and we think this intention makes us stand out."

Doña is the physical representation of the work of its co-founders. The pair created an excellent brand of mezcal, Dangerous Don. They have helped organize London Mezcal Week and are the brains behind Slap Ya Papa, a New Orleans-inspired promoter of live music and food. In Doña, you get live music, comedy nights, drag-queen showcases, and plenty more on most nights.

Of course, the cocktails—all named after women—are also worth sipping. The namesake Doña consists of Dangerous Don, ginger, lime, and white vermouth, while the Sabrina packs a spicy punch with pink peppercorn and habanero shrub.

London roving taco specialists Tigre Tacos provide tasty accompaniments to the proceedings with a variety of fish and veggie tacos available.

FIORELLA

Named after co-founder Lucia Massey's mother, this is essentially a mezcal Martini, reimagined with the house mezcal and served with a little citrus. Feel free to pop in an olive or cornichon for a little bit of an extra briny touch.

1 ¼ oz. Dangerous Don Espadin

½ oz. dry vermouth

½ oz. Italicus

10 drops Empirical Ayuuk

Lemon and/or lime rind twist, to garnish

1. Combine all of the ingredients in a mixing glass filled with ice and stir until chilled.

2. Strain into a chilled cocktail glass.

3. Garnish with the lemon and/or lime rind.

SOUTH LONDON

Formerly an industrial zone filled with tanneries and warehouses, South London is now a checkerboard of radically different areas, united only by their location south of the Thames. The South Bank, for example, is a favorite with locals and tourists alike, providing easy access to the London Eye, The Globe Theater, and the Tate Modern. Dulwich resembles a fairy-tale English village. Brixton and Peckham are vibrant cultural melting pots.

The bars listed here are a rich reflection of this variety—the one thing they have in common are quality drinks.

South London

A. Sugar Kane Bar
247 Lavender Hill

B. Royal Vauxhall Tavern
372 Kennington Ln

C. Lyaness
20 Upper Ground

D. Aqua Shard
31 Thomas St

E. Nine Lives
8 Holyrood St

F. Funkidory
42 Peckham Rye

SUGAR CANE BAR

247 Lavender Hill, London SW11 1JW
Nearest Tube stop: Clapham Junction

Sugar Cane may be small but it packs in loads of Polynesian pop culture via the décor. Sip your cocktail in a private straw hut or find yourself in a cave lavishly decorated with straw chief chairs, exotic flowers, and banana leaves. The tiki theme is woven into everything—even the cocktail glasses.

Be prepared for a wide selection of rum-based cocktails, including the Zombie, where the ingredients aren't on the menu—instead it reads: "Only 2 per person—a clue to this drink's strength!"

A wide range of food also is on the menu, including tapas and burgers as well as the tiki brunch, which includes unlimited rum punch for two hours. As for events, if you're sick of Tinder, speed-dating nights define most Tuesdays and Thursdays while cocktail masterclasses are scheduled every day. For larger groups, book in advance to avoid disappointment—especially if you'd like your own private straw hut.

MAI TAI TWIST AKA FLYING PIG

A unique cocktail originally made for the June 2019 Tiki Love Party hosted in Sugar Cane, it is now immortalized in these pages.

1 ½ oz. Appleton Estate 12 Year Old

2 teaspoons Wray & Nephew Overproof Rum

½ oz. Grand Marnier

2 teaspoons passion fruit puree

2 teaspoons orgeat

2 teaspoons honey

2 teaspoons fresh lime juice

2 dashes Angostura Bitters

1 dash Orange Angostura Bitters

2 dried pineapple slices and passion fruit slice, to garnish

1. Combine all of the ingredients in a cocktail shaker with ice, shake vigorously, and strain into an old-fashioned glass over crushed ice.

2. Garnish with 2 dried pineapple slices and a passion fruit slice.

THE ROYAL VAUXHALL TAVERN

372 Kennington Ln, London, SE11 5HY
Nearest Tube stop: Oval

The Royal Vauxhall Tavern (RVT) is one of London's most important and historically significant LGBTQ+ spaces. Built between 1860 and 1862, since World War II it has hosted drag shows, and in the 1980s it became an iconic gay gathering place—known as The Palladium of Drag until the 1990s—and has served as a bar, theater, and club ever since. In 2015, the RVT became a historically-listed building due to its contribution to LGBTQ+ culture.

And what a space. A sumptuous intimate cabaret bar hosts cabaret and comedy shows, live music, theater, club nights, and more. Something special is on most nights. It has been regularly used as a set for scores of movies, including Goodbye Gemini (1970), Pride (2014), Absolutely Fabulous (2016), and more.

While there's a history of A-listers making appearances here over the years, perhaps the most well known, if not 100 percent corroborated, legend is that Princess Diana visited the bar dressed as a man, accompanied by Freddie Mercury, DJ Kenny Everett, and actress Cleo Rocos. Allegedly, she passed unrecognized as attention was heaped on the rest of the party.

More LGBTQ+ Bars

Looking for spots guaranteed to be inclusive?
Look no further than these welcoming bars.

ABOVE THE STAG
72 Albert Embankment, SE1 7TP

THE COCK TAVERN
340 Kennington Rd, SE11 4LD

FRIENDLY SOCIETY
79 Wardour St, W1D 6QB

G-A-Y BAR
30 Old Compton St, W1D 4UR

NEW BLOOMSBURY SET
76a Marchmont St, WC1N 1AG

THE OLD SHIP STEPNEY
17 Barnes St, E14 7NW

RETRO BAR
2 George Ct, WC2N 6HH

TWO BREWERS
114 Clapham High St, SW4 7UJ

VILLAGE SOHO
81 Wardour St, W1D 6QD

ZODIAC BAR & CLUB
119 Hampstead Rd, NW1 3EE

LYANESS

20 Upper Ground, London, SE1 9PD
Nearest Tube stop: Blackfriars

Bar entrepreneur Ryan Chetiyawardana (also known as Mr. Lyan) played a clever trick when he shuttered his award-winning riverfront bar Dandelyan with its perfect view over the Thames. Hardcore drinks fans were relieved when he simply reopened it with slightly new interiors and colors, renamed as Lyaness. Since then, it has been rightly hailed as one of the world's best bars—just as Dandelyan was.

The made-to-order furniture by Jacu Strauss contributes to the atmosphere of understated, high-end luxury. But the drinks are the star of the show. The cocktail menu is regularly changed and the recipes showcase specific ingredients that might be developed with collaborators or researched and sourced by a member of the Lyaness team. For example, at the time of writing, they include oyster honey, blood curacao, green sauce liqueur, malt and grass amazake, and fruit furikake.

For the ultimate London drinking experience, though, sip the bar's Spirited Tea, a special English teatime experience, featuring three paired cocktails to accompany your brew and nibbles.

Don't be afraid to ask for something slightly more improvised: a made-up whisky cocktail with a splash of sherry is still one of the best I've ever had.

BLOODY MARGARITA

While this clearly references the classic drink, it also adds in a mineral edge that usually comes from the salt (in this case, that's the pig's blood in the house-made curacao; but you can use store-bought), and adds an earthy depth and richer body than is usually found in the drink.

1 oz. blanco tequila

⅞ oz. curaçao

1 teaspoon Cointreau

⅔ oz. fresh lime juice

¼ oz. gomme syrup

Lime wedge, to garnish

1. Combine all of the ingredients in a cocktail shaker with ice, shake well, and double strain into a rocks glass over ice.

2. Garnish with a lime wedge.

AQUA SHARD

Level 31, The Shard, 31 Thomas St,
London, SE1 9RY
Nearest Tube stop: London Bridge

Though you have to submit yourself to an airport-style security scan to get in, the inconvenience is worth it. Aqua Shard, located on the 31st floor of London's tallest building, boasts extraordinary views of the city accentuated by the venue's expansive space and high ceiling. Most major London landmarks are on view, and as day turns to night the light show provided by the city is truly spectacular. The winding Thames is revealed as the city's artery, and trains crisscross the city like model toys.

Walls facing out in three directions are simply made of glass windows framed in steel. If you go at the right time, you can get a table next to a steep drop. Hence, booking in advance is recommended. The cocktail list, inspired by the basic elements of fire, water, air, and earth, isn't shabby either and there's a healthy, if expensive, Champagne list. This ambitious drinking experience isn't cheap. But is it worth it? Absolutely.

And finally, bizarre as it sounds, make sure you visit the toilets. They take full advantage of Aqua Shard's lofty heights. They simply are the best I have ever visited.

NINE LIVES

8 Holyrood St, London, SE1 2AL
Nearest Tube stop: London Bridge

You'll find this subterranean neighborhood bar hidden by London Bridge's arches. A drinks menu inspired by California's laid-back, sunny vibes strives to banish England's typically rainy climate with a space dominated by bamboo, wicker chairs, and hanging plants while retaining a minimalist Scandinavian design.

However, Nine Lives stands out particularly for its commitment to sustainability, both as a business and with cocktails that often use waste ingredients from discarded food and drinks. Bamboo straws eliminate plastic. Owner Allan Gage is also picky about how he designs the recipes for his drinks: "We use carefully selected ingredients that are local, seasonal, or are made by companies that share the same sustainable ethos as us to make bold, delightful twists on classics."

A perfect example: the bar's use of Discarded Spirits's banana rum infused with discarded banana peels in its Tropicalifornication cocktail, featured here.

The outdoor pedestrian cobbled area by the bar, Nine Lives Alley, serves not only a different set of cocktails but also tacos from Tigre Tacos, Nine Lives's resident taco truck.

However, the jewel in Nine Lives crown is its custom sound system. Built by Wave Research, it features four custom WR 322 full-range speakers providing quadrophonic audio. Booze, food, and tunes. These folks have it covered.

TROPICALIFORNICATION

Nine Lives founder Allan Gage says: "This title track removes your shoes, polishes your shades, fans you with a giant palm leaf, and whispers 'Born to Chill' in your ear."

⅞ oz. Discarded Banana Rum

⅞ oz. Pineapple Plantation Rum

2 dashes Angostura Bitters

⅔ oz. fresh lime juice

1 egg white

½ oz. rich simple syrup

Lime zest, to garnish

1. Combine all of the ingredients in a cocktail shaker, dry shake, add ice, and shake again.

2. Strain into a thin double rocks glass over cubed ice and garnish with lime zest.

FUNKIDORY

42 Peckham Rye, London, SE15 4JR
Nearest Tube stop: Peckham Rye (Overground)

Take a wander down the vibrant and diverse South London neighborhood of Peckham for insight into what makes London great. Buses will almost run you over as African and Middle Eastern shops sell an endless selection of imported wares. Let mouthwatering Jamaican food stalls tempt you while street preachers armed with megaphones attempt to save your soul. At the bottom end of Peckham, you will find Funkidory.

It began as a labor of love for couple Sergio Leanza and Anna Fairhead. The small neighborhood bar slowly and steadily grew a loyal clientele of locals thanks to its delicious drinks, welcoming atmosphere, and excellent funk tunes played on vinyl.

Word spread and the critical accolades and awards followed. However, the enterprising couple hasn't let the attention go to their heads: they still regularly work behind the bar.

During the pandemic, Funkidory pivoted and became a combination record-and-booze shop, specializing in natural wines, with an additional bottled-cocktail delivery service. The records and wine are still available, and the wines are now available by the glass, too.

Funkidory's cocktails are just as unforgettable, often inspired by music, Peckham's local history, and its immigrant community. Ingredients from local businesses —such as mead from neighbors Gosnells—are often incorporated. (Sergio became close friends with be-mused Nigerian greengrocers as he hunted for African fruits and malt drinks.)

All in all, it is the perfect intimate urban lounge celebrating Peckham's heritage.

RYE LANE

Based on a Manhattan, one of Funkidory's most popular cocktails has its powerful ingredients pulling this drink in many different directions to achieve a full-bodied and slightly savory result.

1 ½ oz. rye whiskey

⅔ oz. Sacred English Amber vermouth

½ teaspoon Fennel Seed Syrup (see recipe)

½ teaspoon Sicilian olives brine

An olive, to garnish

1. Add all of the ingredients to a mixing glass with ice, stir, and strain into a frozen cocktail glass.

2. Garnish with a Giarraffa or Nocellara olive.

Fennel Seed Syrup: Combine 17 ½ oz. sugar, 9 oz. water, and 15 grams fennel seeds in a saucepan over low heat and cook until the sugar is completely dissolved, stirring frequently. Remove the pan from heat and let stand, covered, for 30 minutes. Strain and store.

WEST LONDON

One of the global capitals of expensive property and all things fancy, West London has plenty to offer—and you don't necessarily need to be flush with cash to enjoy it. Though areas such as Kensington and Chelsea often live up to the posh stereotype, there's plenty of budget-friendly gems to discover, especially in neighborhoods such as Acton and raucous Notting Hill.

However, aside from a few choice destinations, West London isn't frequented too much by your "typical" tourists, aside from the numerous high-end hotels in the area. The three bars listed here reflect radically different (and successful) approaches to attracting Londoners.

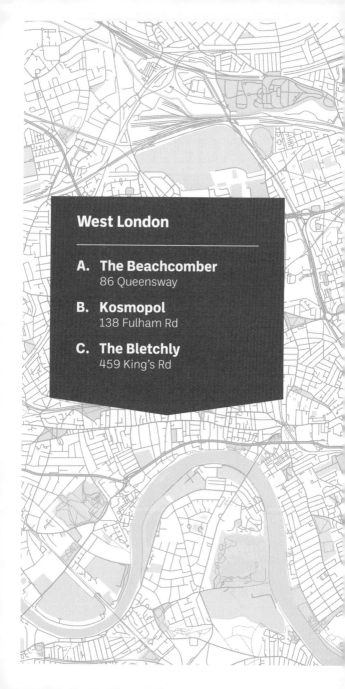

West London

A. **The Beachcomber**
86 Queensway

B. **Kosmopol**
138 Fulham Rd

C. **The Bletchly**
459 King's Rd

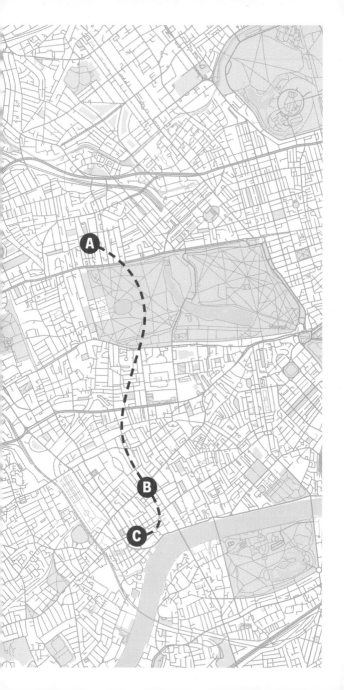

THE BEACHCOMBER

86 Queensway, London, W2 3RR
Nearest Tube stop: Bayswater

Located in the Caribbean-influenced area of Notting Hill, The Beachcomber has the most appropriate location imaginable for a London tiki bar. Emphasizing its tropical island influence, the bar's full name is: The Beachcomber—London's House of Agricole Rhum.

No, the spelling above is not a typo: the "h" in "rhum" signifies a special style of rum produced in the French Caribbean islands. Unlike traditional rums, instead of using the byproduct of sugar production, molasses, rhum agricole is made by directly fermenting and distilling the juice pressed from sugarcane. With the largest selection in the UK, The Beachcomber is certainly the place to taste the difference.

Rattan-clad and banquette-lined, an array of tropically-themed décor has been packed into the small and cozy basement space. A soundtrack that switches between calypso, reggae, and Afro-funk accompanies tiki-style Slings, Hurricanes, and Daquiris. More adventurous options include the Suffering Gringo, a smoky mezcal based-cocktail with a chili kick.

Speaking of chili, the bar actually turns out a strong Thai food menu, too.

KOSMOPOL

138 Fulham Rd, SW10 9PY
Nearest Tube stop: South Kensington

When it first opened 20 years ago, Chelsea-based Kosmopol quickly became known as one of London's top bars, frequented by A-list celebrities and even royalty. Owner Fredrik Olsson swept up the acclaim as he established himself as one of the world's top bartenders.

Over time, however, Olsson became more interested in establishing Kosmopol as the perfect local go-to bar for Chelsea's well-heeled residents: "We pride ourselves on personal high-end service, understanding and listening to our customers' needs. I also understood early that you need to put high focus on the locals who will become your important regulars."

Olsson's Swedish origins are reflected in Kosmopol's tasteful minimalist décor and furnishings and also in the cocktails, some of which have a decidedly Swedish angle and ingredients. One cocktail (recipe below) also features a gin designed by Olsson, with botanicals including cloudberry and pine.

As for the food, while three options are available, I heartily recommend the £3 Swedish hot dog—a delicious bargain that will complement your cocktail, no matter what you're drinking.

SKANDILICIOUS COLLINS

This John Collins variation is given a little extra magic not just by the elderflower cordial but also by using Fredrik Olsson's excellent Skandailicious gin.

1 ¾ oz. Skandilicous Forest Gin

2 teaspoons elderflower cordial

1 teaspoon simple syrup

⅔ oz. fresh lemon juice

Soda water, to top (about 2 oz.)

Dehydrated lemon wheel and a rosemary sprig, to garnish

1. Add the gin, cordial, simple syrup, and lemon juice to a cocktail shaker with ice and shake vigorously.

2. Strain into a highball glass, add ice, top with soda water, and stir to combine.

3. Garnish with a dehydrated lemon slice and a sprig of rosemary.

THE BLETCHLEY

459 King's Rd, London SW10 0LJ
Nearest Tube stop: Chelsea Harbour

Housed in a nineteenth-century Renaissance revival building known as the Chelsea Funhouse, the Bletchley offers a uniquely immersive cocktail experience. Inspired by Alan Turing and his team of World War II cryptographers, be ready for a cocktail-bar-meets-escape-room experience. The result is entertaining, photo friendly, and surprisingly fun, if a tad corny.

Beginning in the secret war room, you must enter your mission codes and decipher messages. If done correctly, these will decode into cocktail ingredients and complex recipes. For those more interested in cocktails than codebreaking, the full menu is available to enjoy while relaxing in the vintage surroundings.

If you're feeling really swanky, you can phone in advance (minimum four days' notice) to order the bar's £100 cocktail, featuring diamonds and edible gold.

No matter what you choose to do, it's impossible not to get lost in the impeccably period-perfect interior. Revel in the feeling of having earned your cocktail—although you may find yourself lingering long after you've broken the code.

WINE BARS

London has a long history of wine, starting with the Romans, who brought wine with them and even attempted to make it during their time in England. Ties with the continent also meant that wine was constantly being imported. For a long time, London was an important wine distribution center, shipping cases to the rest of Britain and around the world.

However, until recently the wine bars and restaurants claiming to take wine seriously in London weren't actually very good. The selection and quality were overall fairly poor.

This has changed radically. You can now find wine bars all over the city devoted to hunting the best bottles and producers. It is easy to find establishments with more than 50 wines on the list, and serious wine joints will have many more than that ready to pour.

Here are the ones that are truly the best of the best in London.

THE REMEDY

124 Cleveland St, London, W1T 6PG
Nearest Tube stop: Great Portland Street

You'll find this tiny bar off of a little backstreet in Fitzrovia, and it's rightly considered to be one of the best locales for drinking wine in London.

With a mission to circumvent what the Remedy team calls the "wine industrial complex," the list here consists entirely of small producers. Though around 100 wines are available, 20 are on a constant weekly rotation and The Remedy also boasts what may be the city's largest selection of orange wines, a type of white wine in which the grape skins are not removed before fermentation.

The food menu is designed to accompany the wine. The menu changes weekly, and everything is made in-house, whenever possible using seasonal ingredients sourced from local producers.

However, in addition to the impeccable service—a refreshing combination of informality and geekiness— you'll often find one of the owners, Renato Catgiu or Andrea Sabbatini, at the bar chatting away with patrons and eagerly making recommendations about wines to try.

THE WHITE HORSE

5 White Horse St, London, W1J 5LQ
Nearest Tube Stop: Green Park

Since its founding in 2012, London wine seller Hedo-nism has become a renowned industry name, selling thousands of bottles of wines and spirits. The White Horse, which opened in the summer of 2021, is its first dedicated bar—the group also operates a Michelin star restaurant, HIDE. "We are a pub with a casual 6,000+ wines to choose from," reads an Instagram-issued boast, although there are usually around 100 available at any time.

Quirky and modern, with large low-hanging bulbs, a marble fireplace, and plenty of candles, it's a stretch to call this transformed abandoned piano bar a pub. That said, this "pub" does serve good beer and shows football matches (soccer games, for the Americans).

The White Horse is the passion project of Hedonism co-owner Tatiana Fokina, who wanted to create a space that could serve as an office for the Hedonism team during the day and convert into a comfy, wine-led drinking establishment at night—meaning that the space could pay for itself.

It's an interesting addition to the Hedonism empire, whose flagship store is flashy and features eye-wateringly expensive bottles. HIDE, both the bar and restaurant, is a truly ambitious gastronomic luxury project. By comparison, The White Horse is a much more intimate and accessible proposition.

CORK AND BOTTLE WINE BAR

44-46 Cranbourn St, London, WC2H 7AN
Nearest Tube stop: Leicester Square

When he moved to London in the early 1970s, flamboyant New Zealander Don Hewitson was shocked to discover that the city's wine bars were in a poor state—double-whammied by bad wines and a limited selection. He launched a campaign to solve this pressing problem, opening many wine bars across the city. His first was Cork and Bottle, which he bought after a year working there. Over the decades, until his death in 2020, Hewitson established himself as one of London's most important wine industry figures.

Cork and Bottle retains his commitment to choice, quality, and quirkiness. Now run by his protégé, Will Clayton, the small subterranean bar has held on to its prime West End location and features a substantial list of 300 bottles from around the world, with a strong emphasis on Australian and New Zealand wines. The cheese options are also impressive, with approximately 15 available at any time to pair accordingly.

However, the signature dish here is the chunky ham-and-cheese pie, with more than 990,000 portions served over a half-century of business since 1971.

LADY OF THE GRAPES

16 Maiden Ln, London, WC2E 7NJ
Nearest Tube stop: Covent Garden

The name of this phenomenal Covent Garden wine bar is apt—Lady of the Grapes highlights wine made primarily by female winemakers. Furthermore, the 200-strong wine list features almost exclusively organic, biodynamic, and natural wines made by small producers.

Parisian owner Carole Bryan, a former art director who decided to change careers, aims to draw attention to the women working in a male-dominated industry as well as the terroir of the wines. The bar itself is a little taste of France in central London, with its rustic décor and impressive display of wine bottles.

The food menu mostly consists of traditional accompaniments to wine, supplemented by a varied list of cheeses and charcuteries. In a nod to its French origins, this is one of the few places in London where you can enjoy buttered snails with garlic if you're feeling adventurous.

The bar also doubles as a shop; wines are available by the bottle alongside a little deli providing cheeses, pâtés, and charcuterie to take home.

GORDON'S WINE BAR

47 Villiers St, London, WC2N 6NE
Nearest Tube stop: Embankment

Housed in a former residence of Rudyard Kipling (which served at another time as a brothel), Gordon's Wine Bar is London's oldest wine bar, owned since 1890 by two unrelated families named Gordon. Three generations of Gordons, all named Angus, worked here until the unrelated Luis Gordon bought the business in 1972. Since his death in 2002, his wife, Wendy, and eldest son, Simon, have run the place.

At Gordon's, forget about cocktails or beer: wine and fortified wine (for example, Madeira, sherry, and port) are the only alcoholic drinks available, both by the glass and bottle. An excellent selection of cheese and charcuterie is available to pair with the wine(s) of your choice.

The bar itself remains virtually unchanged from its nineteenth-century founding aside from the recent addition of an outdoor section, Watergate Walk. Stone walls, candlelit wooden tables, and low, curved cellar walls lend to the Dickensian atmosphere, along with framed historical newspaper clippings and pictures serving as a reminder of Gordon's longevity. G.K. Chesterton and Kipling himself were regulars here, so you can enjoy the bar as they did.

PLUME WINE BAR

26 Wellington St, London, WC2E 7DD
Nearest Tube stop: Covent Garden

Covent Garden is a fascinating neighborhood that blends much of London's contemporary identities. It is quirky, upscale, touristy, and often crowded. It is also full of unique restaurants, cafes, and boutiques, if you can find them beyond the many global brands that have set up shop here, too.

The Plume Wine Bar, formerly Grays and Feather, is one of these gems. When it opened in 2011, Grays and Feather specialized in sparkling and English wines when the latter category was only just starting to be taken a little more seriously. Its wine bar has since been rebranded as Plume, and serves as the showcase space for Grays and Feather's wider work across London, running wine programs for restaurants and street market stalls.

Plume's combination of quirk and class is reflective of Covent Garden. It inhabits what was once Charles Dickens's former publishing house and is spread between two floors. The ground floor combines gentle modern rococo with kooky décor, including a stuffed peacock guarding the stairs to a classy basement area framed around a mural of fanned feathers.

While the wine list is quite good, the main draw is the special and unusual sparkling wines, especially those from England.

NOBLE ROT WINE BAR AND RESTAURANT

51 Lamb's Conduit St, London, WC1N 3NB
Nearest Tube stop: Russell Square

Noble Rot began life as a popular and well-known wine magazine with the admirable goal of making the wine world accessible while avoiding the stereotypical snobbery. In the words of founders Dan Keeling and Mark Andre, the goal of the publication is to "de-twattify" wine. In 2016, they opened a wine bar and restaurant with the same name to immediate critical acclaim and over the years have snared plenty of awards. Among the accolades: the wine list award at the World Restaurant Awards 2019, Wine List of the Year at 2018, 2017, and 2016 National Restaurant Awards, and 2016 Harden's London Restaurant Awards.

There's no snobbery here either. All budgets are catered to—taster glasses start at £3 and prices rise to four figures for certain full bottles. Some wines are also served using the Coravin system, which allows the pouring of wine without opening the bottle and thus stopping the threat of oxidation.

Then there's the food. The menu is designed around the wine. Head chef Tom Upex collaborated with chef Stephen Harris from Michelin-starred restaurant The Sportsman to create a bistro menu combining the best of English and French cuisine, making Noble Rot one of London's ultimate wining-and-dining experiences.

DIOGENES THE DOG

96 Rodney Rd, London, SE17 1BG
Nearest Tube stop: Elephant and Castle

While there are a number of wonderful wine bars across London, it's a bit trickier to find choices south of the Thames. However, just off the busy Walworth Road in Camberwell you'll find this former pub now converted into a classy, dog-friendly wine bar.

Named after the famous Greek cynic philosopher, Diogenes the Dog highlights wines from unusual places, such as China, Bulgaria, Texas, India, and Poland—and also sources many of its bottles directly from producers. The wine list itself isn't large but regularly rotates in new bottles and the bar even has its own custom house wines.

Owner Sunny Hodge also acts as a wine missionary for the neighborhood. Diogenes offers a wine delivery service (with some bottles substantially cheaper than those found at other online retailers), as well as a monthly or weekly subscription club. The bar hosts a variety of wine tastings for private groups, with themes such as unusual wine regions or orange wines.

This hands-on approach has earned the bar a collection of awards and the small space is regularly crowded. You guessed it: advance reservations are highly encouraged.

HOTEL BARS

While the precursor for cocktails begins in London's Victorian gin palaces of the nineteenth century, the city's hotels refined them into the drinks we recognize today.

London, in particular, was, and still is, one of the world's leading cities for cocktails, and many classic recipes were first developed in hotel bars, some which are still in business. For example, Harry Craddock's 1930s *Savoy Cocktail Book*, developed during his time as head bartender at the Savoy Hotel near Covent Garden, is a must-read for any aspiring bartender, and introduced many drinks that are now staples at most bars. Little surprise that the cocktails you'll find in many London hotel bars will blow you away as a result.

The bars featured in this chapter are in general pretty fancy places though—and the drinks will be some of the most expensive in the city. They're worth the money.

A

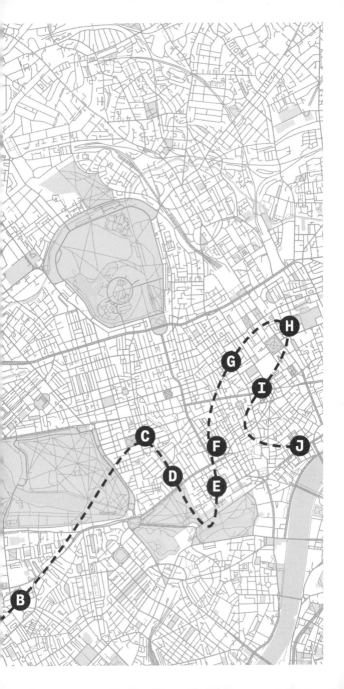

MELODY WHISKY BAR
AT ST. PAUL'S HOTEL

153 Hammersmith Rd, London, W14 0QL
Nearest Tube stop: Barons Court

The Melody Whisky Bar stands out not just for its excellent selection of whiskies and lovely décor but for its fair prices. This was a conscious decision by the team, according to whisky specialist Joel Luumi: "Many whiskies have rapidly increasing value. We try to purchase these and open them on the bar at a fair markup based on the cost rather than the secondary value. Many of our customers have come to appreciate the opportunity to try whiskies which they might have missed due to high demand."

A great way to work through Melody's whisky collection is to partake of one of a wide selection of tasting flights. Five small measures of 10 ml (⅜ oz.) are poured—a perfect way to try different whiskies without either spending or drinking too much. For example, the Around the World flight takes you to five different countries for £15 and a flight specializing in Weller's is priced at £20. There are single-cask flights, regional flights, new distillery flights—the options go on and on. The result is a delight for whisky newbies and geeks alike, and the cocktails are quite tasty, too.

A regular stream of whisky dinner nights pairing the bar's whiskies with the restaurant's food show how whisky can be just as good as wine with a meal.

SPEY CHOCOLATE

If the whisky has got the word "cacao" in its name, then it's begging to be used in a chocolate-oriented cocktail. Adding the Borghetti helps turn this into a little bit more of a mocha-oriented cocktail.

1 ½ oz. The Macallan Harmony Collection Rich Cacao

⅞ oz. Antica Formula

1 oz. Borghetti

5 dashes chocolate bitters

Grated dark chocolate, to garnish

1. Combine all of the ingredients in a cocktail shaker with ice, shake well, and strain into a coupe.

2. Garnish with grated dark chocolate.

ESQ BAR
AT 100 QUEENS GATE HOTEL

100 Queens Gate, London, SW7 5AG
Nearest Tube stop: South Kensington

The 100 Queens Gate Hotel served as the home of Victorian aristocrat William Alexander and the whole facility leans heavily into this theme. As a result, ESQ Bar resembles a Victorian British parlor room. Various tchotchkes and curios are scattered throughout the space accompanied by elaborate carpeting and wooden carvings, making the bar extremely Instagram friendly.

However, ESQ's main calling card are the homemade infused spirits created by its mixology team. Exploring the options is part of the fun of coming here, and the bartending team is happy to create a bespoke cocktail featuring an ingredient that piques your curiosity. A pan-Asian nibbles and small-plates food menu helps line the stomach.

While live music echoes on Friday and Saturday nights, early evening may be the best time for a drink so you can check out the self-playing grand piano, one of the few you'll find in a London bar.

149

CONNAUGHT BAR
AT CONNAUGHT HOTEL

The Connaught, Carlos Pl, London, W1K 2AL
Nearest Tube stop: Bond Street

This is the best bar in the world. This isn't my opinion but that of the leading award body, World's 50 Best Bars. The Connaught Bar successfully defended its title of World's Best Bar in 2021, and it was near the top before that.

The Connaught Bar's success is largely due to Italian Agostino "Ago" Perrone, who has recruited, trained, and shaped a phenomenal team of elite bartenders since the relaunch of the bar 13 years ago, following an extensive refurb that resulted in a plush setting with green leather couches, marbled tables, and sumptuous paneling.

It is no exaggeration to say that the Connaught Bar is the bar equivalent of a three-star Michelin restaurant. Luxury and impeccable service are combined with irresistible aromas and flavors from incredible cocktails, each one a unique gem.

However, any drinking experience at the Connaught Bar should start with its Martini, which Perrone has made the symbol of the Connaught's approach to service and outstanding quality. A gorgeous golden trolley is wheeled out with a choice of aromatic bitters used in your drink. My last visit afforded a selection of cardamom, lavender, licorice, grapefruit, vanilla, ginger, and coriander seed bitters. Whatever you pick, it will be liquid perfection.

CONNAUGHT MARTINI

Though you won't make this as well as the Connaught Bar team does, feel free to get creative with the bitters, and remember to use a chilled cocktail glass!

½ oz. dry vermouth (the bar uses a blend)

2 ½ oz. gin or vodka (Tanqueray No. Ten is one of the bar's preferred gins)

5 drops bitters (use whatever bitters you like best)

Lemon twist or olive, to garnish

1. Chill a cocktail glass.
2. Add the vermouth and chosen spirit to a mixing glass filled with ice and stir until chilled.
3. Coat the chilled glass with the bitters and then strain the cocktail into the glass, with as much distance as possible between the mixing glass and the cocktail glass.
4. Garnish with a lemon twist or an olive.

THE BLUE BAR
AT THE BERKELEY

The Berkeley, Wilton Pl, London, SW1X 7RL
Nearest Tube stop: Hyde Park Corner

The Blue Bar was the celebrity hangout when it first opened in 2000, with notables such as Madonna and John Galliano rapturously singing its praises. More than 20 years later, it is still a cutting-edge cocktail bar considered to be one of the city's best and visited by many well-heeled Londoners.

As the name implies, it is also very blue. Specifically, it is Lutyen's Blue, which comes close to light purple. Designer David Collins created the specific shade in honor of the original architect of the Berkeley's old site at Piccadilly Circus, Edwin Lutyens, who designed some of the carvings that were moved from there into this room. Collins protégé Roger Angell kept the color scheme, carvings, and art deco feel in a 2016 renovation.

As for the drinks, the current "meta menu" serves vibrant colors while the cocktails themselves are grouped into four flavor categories: fresh, bubbly, crisp, and bold.

DUKES BAR
AT DUKES LONDON HOTEL

DUKES London, 33 St. James Pl,
London, SW1A 1NY
Nearest Tube stop: Green Park

Despite its setting in a fancy hotel, the classy and lush DUKES Bar isn't easy to find, hidden in a dead-end alleyway. That hasn't proved an obstacle for an endless stream of patrons who frequent it. . . frequently. Though it is a top-end cocktail bar, the world-famous Martinis are the main draw for many drinkers.

For more than 15 years, bar manager Alessandro Palazzi has been responsible for ensuring his crew of white-jacketed staff maintains impeccable standards. The Martini ingredients arrive on trolleys and aren't served with ice—the glasses are chilled in a freezer along with the gin or vodka. They're also strong, with five shots of alcohol per Martini, and beautifully garnished with Amalfi lemon peels. The formal rule is that no customer is allowed a third Martini—they are simply too strong.

There's another historical reason to imbibe a Martini here: James Bond creator Ian Fleming was a regular and it is possibly where he came up with the idea of the Vesper Martini that was first introduced in 1953 via the first Bond book, *Casino Royale*.

Even English royalty is addicted to these martinis. In a 2021 interview, Jack Brooksbank, the husband of Queen Elizabeth II's granddaughter, Princess Eugenie, revealed that a secret passage connects St. James Palace to the bar.

DUKE'S BAR CLASSIC MARTINI

There's two Martini recipes in this book sourced from two of the world's best Martini bars. Only one way to find out which is your favorite. It's safe to say this is the stronger one of the two. Remember to really chill both the gin and the glass.

3 dashes Sacred English Dry Vermouth

4 oz. gin, frozen

Lemon peel, to garnish

1. Add the vermouth to the frozen cocktail glass and coat the glass.

2. Pour in the gin. Don't stir.

3. Garnish with a lemon peel.

THE GREEN BAR
AT HOTEL CAFÉ ROYAL

Hotel Café Royal, 15 Glasshouse St,
London, W1B 4DY
Nearest Tube stop: Piccadilly Circus

This is a historic London location. Before it was relaunched as a hotel in 2012, the old Café Royal served for more than a century as a gathering place for some of the world's most famous people. Well-known guests have included Oscar Wilde, Virginia Woolf, Winston Churchill, Elizabeth Taylor, Mick Jagger, Muhammad Ali, and Princess Diana, to name a few.

Many of the Green Bar's drinks come from the *Café Royal Cocktail Book*, first compiled in 1937. Among other advantages, this is the prime destination for the ultimate flavored G&T. Expert bartenders can help you choose from an assortment of 18 gins to partner with seven different tonics. Classic cocktail offerings, small plates, and lunch dishes are also available.

Other than the G&T, the Green Bar is one of London's top venues for the ultimate absinthe experience—the inspiration behind the bar's name. A favorite of bohemian intellectuals of an era long gone, the bar features a fountain flowing with a steady drizzle of the green fairy's finest.

This 1920s Brutalist-inspired building is the place to relive the classic era of cocktail indulgence. Wednesday and Thursday evenings are the best time to come here—that's when the top-quality live jazz is on.

THE PUNCH ROOM
AT THE LONDON
EDITION

10 Berners St, London, W1T 3NP
Nearest Tube stop: Oxford Circus/Tottenham
Court Road

Historically, punches—communal fruit-based drinks (usually alcoholic) served out of a large bowl—were introduced by employees of the East India Company. The word very likely first emerged from the Hindi word "paanch," which means "five," representing the five ingredients typically used: spirits, water, lemon juice, sugar, and spice.

The Edition Hotel's Punch Room takes things a little further. Here you'll find 30 different specialty punches, all of them with many more than five ingredients and served in portions for one, two, four, six, or eight people. It is the most extensive punch list in the city. While they are rotated, each punch exemplifies a careful, many layered balance of component ingredients. Of course, certain classics are always available, like the Milk Punch, featured here.

Tucked away behind an unassuming door past the main hotel lobby bar, the Punch Room is available only by advance reservation. It's worth the effort. The sumptuous oak-paneled room evokes an Edwardian manor, and the hardback menus ooze class.

LONDON EDITION MILK PUNCH

One of the bar's classic punches, this is the perfect drink to prepare the day before a house party or dinner. The mix of the ingredients may seem strange but they come together beautifully.

21 oz. pineapple

6 cloves

1 piece star anise

¼ tablespoon allspice

Coriander seeds to taste

10 oz. Cognac

10 oz. Somerset Cider Brandy

14 oz. lemon sherbet (or sorbet)

7 oz. Blackwell Rum

7 oz. Plantation Barbados Rum

7 oz. Arak

7 oz. green tea (milk oolong tea is best)

28 oz. boiling water

28 oz. milk

2 oz. fresh lemon juice

Pineapple slices, to garnish

1. In a large bowl, muddle the spices and the pineapple.

2. Add all of the liquids, except the milk and lemon juice, to the bowl, hot water last. Steep for six hours.

3. Once steeped, boil the milk, and then add it and the lemon juice into the punch mixture. Strain to remove solids.

4. Refrigerate overnight and strain again.

5. Serve over one large ice cube and garnish each glass with a pineapple slice.

FITZ'S BAR
AT KIMPTON FITZROY

Russell Square, London, WC1B 5BE
Nearest Tube stop: Russell Square

This high-end hotel bar is named after Charles Fitzroy Doll, architect of The Principal London Hotel (now the Kimpton Fitzroy) where the bar is located. It's split between two spaces. The main bar area, the Mural Room, features an eighteenth-century stained-glass window, modern art, and plush seats. The other space, The Mirrorball Room, requires an advance reservation and combines Jazz Age decadence with a disco party. A large fireplace is set off by crocodile skin wallpaper. "The place if Rick James and Jay Gatsby threw a bash," goes the official description. Somehow, the result delivers that claim.

A nibbles menu provides a variety of flavors to accompany the drinks, ranging from quail Scotch egg to a Reuben sandwich and teriyaki oyster mushrooms. The spirits menu is healthy and varied, and the cocktails aspire to create multisensory experiences derived from colors and how they are typically perceived, alternating shades in playful experiments.

If you're ready to explore the creations of Fitz's excellent bar team, also be ready to spend a little more than usual, even by London standards.

THE CORAL ROOM
AT THE BLOOMSBURY

16-22 Great Russell St, London, WC1B 3NN
Nearest Tube stop: Tottenham Court Road

This is a truly regal bar. Designed by legendary interior designer Martin Brudnizki, the Coral Room reaches for art deco glory further highlighted by the space's coral-pink walls. Add the mirrors, chandeliers, and art by Luke Edward Hall and the result is a classy salon that happens to serve excellent cocktails.

There are two options. The bar team—led by respected bar manager Giovanni Spezziga—keeps the classic cocktails simple and does them well using excellent ingredients. Then there is a selection of more creative and elaborate drinks inspired by England's iconic locations.

Speaking of English-inspired drinks, make sure you examine the selection of English sparkling wines, which is one of the most extensive in the country. There's even a specially-made vintage from East Sussex producer Ridgeview named after the Bloomsbury.

Bear in mind, though, that none of this comes cheap—this is a fancy London hotel bar after all—but the steep prices are worth it.

GIN LANE

Named after a famous mid-eighteenth-century print by William Hogarth warning of society's collapse due to gin consumption, this is a fresh, floral, and tangy delight that ignores Hogarth's warning.

1 ¾ oz. Viognier

1 oz. Hendrick's Gin

2 teaspoons St-Germain

2 teaspoons Monin Rose Syrup

1 teaspoon agave nectar

Dehydrated rosebud, to garnish

1. Chill a cocktail glass.
2. Add all of the ingredients to a mixing glass filled with ice and stir until chilled.
3. Strain into the chilled glass and garnish with the dehydrated rosebud.

THE GIN PALACE
AT STRAND PALACE

372 Strand, London, WC2R 0JJ
Nearest Tube stop: Charing Cross/Temple/
Covent Garden

A perfect stop for a drink while wandering around central London, located a short walk from Trafalgar Square just off the Strand.

A recent relaunch of The Gin Palace keeps things simple, relaxed, and classy. While they are pricey, the Gin and Tonic selection here is lovely, mixing a variety of gins with flavored sodas from Franklin & Sons. Feel free to mix and match your own.

The cocktail menu mixes impeccably made classics with more original gin-based creations—the Aurora (see recipe) blends prosecco, gin, fig liqueur, and basil very nicely, while the Coley takes a Negroni into new territory, thanks to the innovative ingredients used: quince gin, Amaro Averna, Lillet Rosé, and some orange bitters.

If you're looking for a top-end boozy tea experience, head over to the Strand Palace's tea room, where a gin or Prosecco cocktail with tea and marmalade in it accompanies your scones, treats, and loose-leaf teas.

AURORA

This is a multilayered drink with a little bit of everything happening at once. Herbal notes emerge from the basil, indulgent richness from the fig liqueur, a bit of strength from the gin, and sparkles from the Prosecco.

1 ¼ oz. Tanqueray No. 10 Gin

⅔ oz. fig liqueur

½ oz. fresh lime juice

5 fresh basil leaves

Prosecco, to top

Grapefruit peel, to garnish

1. Slap the basil leaves (it releases aromatics) and mix them with the gin, fig liqueur, and lime juice in a shaker filled with ice and shake.
2. Fine strain into a coupe and top the drink with prosecco.
3. Garnish with the grapefruit peel.

PUBS

Short for the term "public house," which emerged in the late seventeenth century, Samuel Pepys described pubs back then as "the heart of England." Unfortunately, pubs are slowly becoming an endangered species. According to the UK Office of National Statistics, more than 11,000 pubs were shut down between 2008 and 2018. The pandemic certainly hasn't helped this figure either.

However, the pub remains a venerated institution across the UK and the best ones serve as hubs for local communities to come together and enjoy a few good drinks, usually pints of beer.

In modern times, pubs are often throwbacks to an earlier age, and while there are pubs in London that have been in business for many centuries, pubs as we typically imagine them—featuring wooden structures and facades, bar counters, brass fittings, and hand pumps—mostly emerged in the nineteenth century.

It is also important to note that these days most pubs are actually owned by large "pubco" corporate conglomerates that hire a designated publican to operate them. While this is the case for some of the pubs featured in this chapter, most of the ones highlighted are still proudly independent and serve excellent drinks.

A

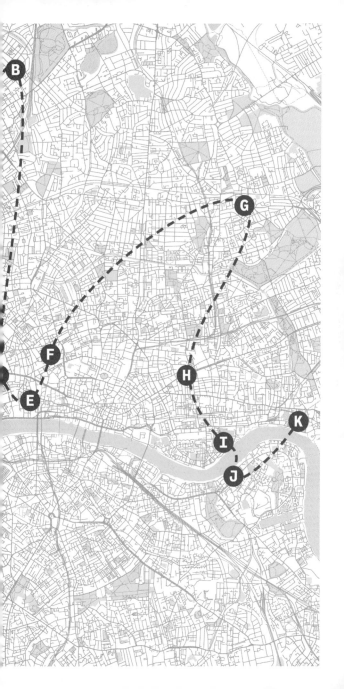

THE CHAMPION

12-13 Wells St, London, W1T 3PA
Nearest Tube stop: Tottenham Court Road

The Champion, dating back to the 1860s, is now an establishment typical of its conglomerate owner, Sam Smith, a chain of pubs found throughout the UK. A perfectly passable gastropub with a Victorian-era feel, it serves beers made at the large Samuel Smith's brewery. This one happens to be located in the center of London in Fitzrovia, next to the shopping mecca of Oxford Street.

So why is it included in this book? The answer is simple: the windows. The stunning stained-glass windows installed throughout the pub feature portraits of "champions" from the Victorian era. These include sporting champions such as cricket player WG Grace, boxer Bob Fitzsimmons, jockey Fred Archer, and Matthew Webb, the first person to swim unaided across the English Channel. Other important figures are nursing pioneer Florence Nightingale, climber Matthew Whymper, and explorer David Livingstone.

Although they may look like they were installed long ago, the windows actually were made by artist Ann Sotheran and installed in 1989. They help make The Champion seem like a little booze-based chapel, a perfect place to escape the nearby crowds.

THE FALTERING FULLBACK

19 Perth Rd, Finsbury Park, London N4 3HB
Nearest Tube stop: Finsbury Park

This well-loved Irish pub has many cards up its sleeve. Inside, the décor is in line with many of the pubs in Dublin's Temple Bar but with additional quirks, such as bicycles and musical instruments suspended from the ceiling. It has two bars, a large back room, and a pool table, indicative of the bar's passion for showing an array of sports, from football to hurling.

However, the real gem here is the beer garden, so covered in ivy and other plants that you will feel lost in a forest. Get here early for a prime spot in the multitiered tree house.

A visit to the Faltering Fullback offers many activities, such as live acoustic music at the front bar, alternating between traditional Irish folk and busker singer-songwriters. In the back room, on Thursdays from 9 p.m., local artists perform in a variety of styles and genres. A Monday pub quiz takes place starting at 8:45 p.m., offering cash prizes to the winning team.

A somewhat surprising feature is the food on the menu, covering an impressive array of authentic Thai food served in the evening.

THE LAMB

94 Lamb's Conduit St, London WC1N 3LZ
Nearest Tube stop: Russell Square

Built in the 1720s, this pub was refurbished in the Victorian era and has been frequented by famous figures such as Charles Dickens, Ted Hughes, and his wife, Sylvia Plath. The bar provides a chance to see a rare and well-preserved example of a "snob screen": etched glass panes with a movable wooden compartment, designed for the middle-class drinkers to see the staff and working-class drinkers in the adjoining bar, but not to be seen in return. If you're lucky, you may come across the bar's old Polyphone—a Victorian mechanical device serving as the jukebox of its day, which, purportedly, still works.

Both pub classics and innovative signature dishes feature on the menu, offering the quintessential British pub experience with a combination of quality dining. Sunday roasts are a must.

While private hire, large bookings, and sit-down meals can be enjoyed upstairs, this is your choice if you're looking for a well-preserved example of a Victorian London pub, which also has a sizeable beer garden. Order a Youngs traditional ale or a selection of rotating guest beers on tap.

THE SHIP TAVERN

12 Gate St, London, WC2A 3HP
Nearest Tube stop: Holborn

The Ship's origins are religious in nature. It was founded in 1549 during the short reign of Henry VIII's teenage son, Edward VI. A staunch Protestant, he outlawed the Catholic Mass. As a result, Mass and other ceremonies were held in secret behind the bar. If the authorities were spotted in the area, the congregation would hide the rosaries and pick up pints to camouflage their activities.

Like some of the historic pubs featured in this book, and across the UK, the modern Ship Tavern has a black façade and its name in gold lettering, surrounded by flowers hung in baskets. It's warm and friendly, tastefully paneled, and the main bar splits the seating into booths, encouraging privacy and intimacy. The upstairs restaurant features mahogany walls and an open fireplace.

Most important though, the food and drinks are excellent. There's the traditional pub fare (think: pies and fish-and-chips) while the restaurant is more of a classy British bistro. Plenty of excellent ales are on draft. Beyond beer, the wine list isn't shabby. But gin holds pride of place here, with over 60 on offer.

YE OLDE CHESHIRE CHEESE

146 Fleet St, London, EC4A 2BP
Nearest Tube stop: Blackfriars

One of London's and the UK's most iconic pubs, this is an ancient institution: a pub has held this site since 1538. This current iteration spread between four floors is one of the pubs that was rebuilt after the Great Fire of London in 1666.

Though situated in a protected historic building located in a tiny alley, Ye Olde Cheshire Cheese oozes shabby class, and it really does feel like entering through a time portal that goes back 100 years. Dim lighting and the smell of an open fire may seem disorienting, but that's part of the fun as you explore its nooks, crannies, and alcoves. Steep stone staircases lead to the different areas of the bar, including the basement vaults that survived the fire and which are the oldest sections of the building.

Fleet Street was once home to most of London's journalists and hacks, so the pub has long been popular with them. Many writers also frequented the Cheese, including Sir Arthur Conan Doyle, G.K. Chesterton, Mark Twain, and Charles Dickens. It is mentioned or alluded to in numerous nineteenth-century classics. It also likely served as a brothel in the middle of the previous century.

However, the Cheese's most famous regular wasn't human. Polly the Parrot, renowned for his ability to swear at customers and mimic all kinds of sounds, including popping champagne corks, held court here for 40 years, until his death from old age in 1926. His obituary was published in 200 international newspapers, but you can still visit him where he sits, stuffed, in a glass case at the Cheese.

YE OLDE MITRE

1 Ely Court, Ely Place, London, EC1N 6SJ
Nearest Tube stop: Chancery Lane/Farringdon

It is virtually impossible to find this pub casually, even though it's in the center of London. Slip down a little side alley to enter the courtyard in which it's been located since 1546, when it catered to the servants of the palace of the Bishop of Ely (once upon a time an opulent residence and home to Queen Elizabeth's commoner consort, Christopher Hatton).

Though the palace was demolished in 1776, the pub lives on. Originally built around an old cherry tree previously used as a dancing maypole (rumored to have been a centerpiece for the toe-tapping Elizabeth and Hatton), its remains now form the front façade.

Today, the pub is owned by the Japanese drinks giant Asahi, which operates hundreds of pubs across the UK. However, the Mitre is still a special place. Dark paneling, heavy oak furniture, and Elizabeth I memorabilia add intimate gravitas. It's warm and pleasant, with an upstairs room and covered outdoor patio. All in all, a classically English boozing space.

THE CHESHAM ARMS

East London Public House, 15 Mehetabel Rd,
London E9 6DU
Nearest Tube stop: Hackney Central

This historic pub was saved after its closure in 2012 when the local community successfully campaigned against its residential conversion. Six months after reopening in 2014, it was voted the best pub in the City and East London Area by CAMRA, a nonprofit that supports pubs serving great bear. Its beer garden has also been described as one of the best in London.

The Chesham Arms does the simple things well: sizeable seating areas, with cask ales and ciders on tap, and it doubles as a rare example of a pub that hasn't become a restaurant in disguise. While it lacks a kitchen, its deal with a local pizza company allows you to order pies to the pub, and substantial bar snacks are offered as well.

Expect to find a lit fireplace during the winter months, and children are welcome until 8 p.m. It's dog friendly, too. A shining example of a proper local.

THE BLIND BEGGAR

337 Whitechapel Rd, London, E1 1BU
Nearest Tube stop: Whitechapel

Built in 1894, the Blind Beggar is named after Henry de Montfort, a nobleman who was wounded and lost his sight at the Battle of Evesham in 1265. The legend goes that he was nursed back to health but eventually became a street beggar.

The pub itself, now a legendary London institution, is the site of a few noteworthy moments in London history. The founder of the Salvation Army, William Booth, preached his first open-air sermon outside the building. For much of the twentieth century, it was a place favored by London's underworld. Infamous gangster Ronnie Kray shot and murdered Georgie Cornell in the bar and was eventually sentenced to life in prison for the crime.

Under the ownership of David Dobson since 2005, it now boasts a sizeable beer garden and also offers a "gangster walking tour" with actor Vas Blackwood (he of Guy Ritchie's English crime film *Lock, Stock and Two Smoking Barrels*). He'll walk you around the neighborhood, providing a history of Kray's brutal reign in the area as well as the shooting locations of the film, now considered a classic gangster flick.

In short, this is a lovely pub—and a crucial stop for any true-crime enthusiasts.

THE PROSPECT OF WHITBY

57 Wapping Wall, London, E1W 3SH
Nearest Tube stop: Wapping

On the banks of the Thames, The Prospect of Whitby claims to be Britain's oldest riverside tavern, dating from around 1520. This historically listed building was formerly known as the Devil's Tavern, hinting at its dubious past. Today, however, it's stocked with fine traditional ales, classic pub grub, and roasts every Sunday. The pub is lavishly decorated with nautical-themed items, with a nod to the days when cargo ships docked next door on their way north to Newcastle-upon-Tyne.

It retains some of its old features, such as a pewter-top bar and a 400-year-old stone floor. The façade dates from the nineteenth century while the inner paneling was installed in the eighteenth century.

The interior and quirkiness of the building itself will whisk you back to The Prospect's earlier days. While you enjoy a real ale, explore the main bar, the riverside restaurant, upstairs Smugglers' Bar, and the "secret" garden.

THE MAYFLOWER PUB

117 Rotherhithe St, London, SE16 4NF
Nearest Tube stop: Rotherhithe (Overground)

The story of 102 English pilgrims leaving from Plymouth on the Mayflower for Cape Cod is foundational for any American. However, before Plymouth their journey started from the London port of Rotherhithe, where the ship's captain, Christopher Jones, was based.

It is entirely possible that captain, crew, and maybe even some of the pilgrims had visited this pub, previously named the Spread Eagle, which has been in operation since around 1550. You can spot the Mayflower's original mooring point from the pub's terrace.

The pub itself is a charming and warm space favored by local residents of the quiet Rotherhithe area and nearby Bermondsey. It's characterized by an excellent selection of craft beers and local ales. Framed prints and portraits related to local history crowd the walls and the candlelit dining area is intimate—a quintessential pub doing things just right.

The Mayflower Pub has another unique selling point: it is the only pub licensed to sell UK and US postage stamps, and has been doing so since the 1800s. Buy them at the bar with your pint.

THE GRAPES

76 Narrow St, London, E14 8BP
Nearest Tube stop: Limehouse (DLR)

Standing for almost 500 years, The Grapes is mentioned in the opening chapter of Charles Dickens's *Our Mutual Friend*: "A tavern of dropsical appearance . . . long settled down into a state of hale infirmity."

Its days of infirmity, however, are long gone. Today, it's a warm and welcoming traditional pub-restaurant serving excellent beer and wine, with a small upstairs terrace offering stunning views over the Thames. A popular pub quiz takes place every Monday. The Victorian long bar is complemented by various oil paintings hanging throughout the space, and leads to what is affectionally known as The Dickens Snug, a little area where the great author supposedly danced on the tables on his wilder nights. It boasts his entire collection of work, available for any visitor to read.

So, beyond the Dickens connection, why is there a large wizard's staff behind the bar and a small statue of Gandalf in the upstairs drinking area? Because actor Ian McKellen has been a part owner of The Grapes since 2011, and that staff is one he used while filming the *Lord of the Rings* trilogy.

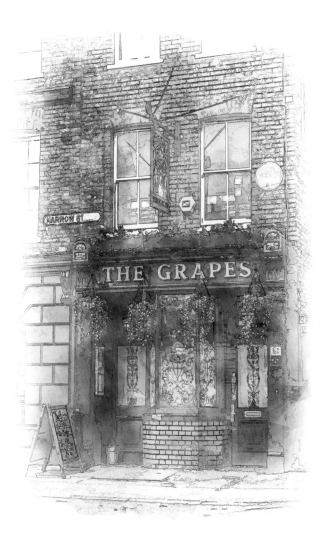

BOOZE MAKERS

From Romans making wine to the Gin Craze that led to a decades-long binge to today, London boasts a rich history of alcohol production and distribution, if not always a very nice one. That said, we are currently in the middle of what you could call a global boom of craft alcohol producers, as the knowledge behind the production of beer, wine, and spirits has become more accessible.

Though there still are some enormous industrial operations such as Beefeater's Gin, most of London's modern booze makers are smaller independent businesses, and they are (mostly) valuing quality over quantity. The individuals behind them come from all kinds of backgrounds. Hayman's Gin, for example, is produced by a family that has been in the gin business for generations, while Taxi Spirits Company, London's first white rum producer, is run by a cab driver who managed to educate himself on distillation while also driving passengers around the city.

The variety of London-made booze is impressive. There are producers making whisky, wine, beer, gin, vodka, vermouth, and plenty more. They are united by a commitment to create truly tasty products and share them with consumers while building a successful business despite the small scales of production, high costs of doing business in London, and competition from bigger players.

A. Bimber
56 Sunbeam Rd

B. Sipsmith
83 Cranbrook Rd

C. Portobello Road Gin
186 Portobello Rd

D. Half Hitch
Camden Lock Pl

E. Hayman's Gin
8A Weir Rd

F. Temple Brew House
46 Essex St

G. Orbit Beers Brewery & Taproom
233 Fielding St

H. Jensen's Gin
55 Stanworth St

I. Renegade Urban Winery
Arch 12 Gales Gardens

J. East London Liquor Company
221 Grove Rd

K. Taxi Spirit Company
St. Paul's Way

BIMBER

56 Sunbeam Rd, London, NW10 6JQ
Nearest Tube stop: North Acton

One of England's best whisky distilleries was born as the dream of third-generation distiller Dariusz Plazewski. It is in such demand with whisky connoisseurs that nearly every release sells out instantly.

This means the best chance of actually tasting Bimber's single malt whiskies is either to find the shops that carry it and get there before it's gone—in order to do this, be sure to join the Bimber Klub where information about new releases can be found—or to visit the distillery for a tour and tasting. The distillery website offers only one very tasty whisky not originally made at Bimber, the Apogee 12 year old, which is a blended whisky that spent a short time undergoing additional maturation in ex-Bimber casks.

Bimber's whiskies generally are intense, full-bodied, and beautifully balanced despite their young age, with all barley sourced from a single farm in Hampshire. However, don't turn your nose up at its gins. The Da Hong Pao Tea Gin is an earthy floral delight and the Kumquat Gin offers bright citrus notes.

BIMBER APOGEE OLD-FASHIONED

The distillery loves serving this classic cocktail to its visitors.

½ teaspoon simple syrup

3 dashes Angostura bitters

1 teaspoon water

1 ¾ oz. Apogee Pure Malt Whisky

Orange peel, to garnish

1. Stir the simple syrup and bitters into a glass with the teaspoon of water until fully blended.

2. Fill the glass with ice, add the whisky, and then gently stir to combine.

3. Express the oil of the orange peel by twisting it over the glass and then drop it in.

SIPSMITH

83 Cranbrook Rd, London, W4 2LJ
Nearest Tube stop: Stamford Brook

The brainchild of boyhood friends Sam Galsworthy and Fairfax Hall and drinks expert and historian Jared Hall, Sipsmith still stands at the vanguard of the latest gin wave that began in the mid-2000s.

After mastering a successful dry gin in 2009, the small Chiswick-based distillery now produces many other flavored gins, including orange and cacao, lemon drizzle, and even a juniper-heavy overproof gin bottled at 57.7% ABV. Leveraging its success and posh West London location, Sipsmith has become the official gin brand of the Wimbledon championships, celebrating the partnership with an official strawberry gin.

As with the other distilleries listed here, tours and tastings are available, as well as cocktail classes where you can make three different cocktails using experimental gins not sold to the general public. The only other way to get these on your palate is to join Sipsmith's Sipping Society (unfortunately, only available to UK residents), where two experimental gins are sent to your mailbox every two months.

To its credit, Sipsmith is one of the most sustainable gin distilleries in the country, achieving B Corp certification—the gold standard of sustainability business—as it reduces carbon emissions, better recycles its packaging materials, and eliminates on-site waste.

STRAWBERRY SMASH SPRITZ

This cocktail was created to celebrate Sipsmith's partnership with the Wimbledon tennis championship as its official gin brand, which also included a strawberry-flavored gin. Strawberries and cream are the iconic snack of the tournament, so they feature heavily here.

1 ¾ oz. Sipsmith Strawberry Smash Gin

⅞ oz. fresh lemon juice

1 ¾ oz. soda water

Prosecco, to top

Fresh sliced strawberry and lime peel twist, to garnish

1. Add the gin, lemon juice, and soda water to a large wine glass filled with ice and stir.

2. Top with chilled prosecco and garnish with sliced strawberry and a lime peel twist.

PORTOBELLO ROAD GIN (THE DISTILLERY)

186 Portobello Rd, London, W11 1LA
Nearest Tube stop: Ladbroke Grove

In 2008, Leeds-based bar entrepreneurs Ged Feltham and Jake Burger threw open the doors of the Portobello Star bar. A few years later, they started wondering what they could do with the two available floors above the venue. Following a tour of the Beefeater distillery, they decided to venture into that business and created a small experimental distillery and gin museum. After perfecting the recipe, they turned to eighth-generation distiller and gin expert Charles Maxwell to increase production. Thus, Portobello Road Gin was born.

In 2016, they opened a new, four-floor facility simply called The Distillery, which is now a gin-imbibing mecca. In addition to a distillery producing gin and vodka, you'll find two bars, a booze shop, a restaurant, and a hotel—all dedicated to eating and drinking well.

Spirits education is also an important component. Gin-making classes are available, during which you make your own special gin, or participate in tasting and cocktail sessions covering a wide selection of spirits. By the way, attend the gin-making class and you can even order bottles of your spirited invention.

CORPSE REVIVER #2

One of the most famous recipes from Harry Craddock's 1930 legendary *Savoy Cocktail Book*, the Corpse Reviver is meant to chase away the hangover from the previous night's drinking. However, as noted in the book: "Four of these taken in swift succession will un-revive the corpse again . . ."

1 dash absinthe

⅞ oz. Portobello Road London Dry Gin

⅞ oz. Cointreau

⅞ oz. Lillet Blanc

⅞ oz. fresh lemon juice

1. Fill a cocktail glass with ice, add the absinthe, swirl it about in the glass, and let stand.
2. Add the remainder of the ingredients to a cocktail shaker with ice, shake well, and strain into the cocktail glass.

HALF HITCH

Unit 53, West Yard, Camden Lock Pl,
London, NW1 8AF
Nearest Tube stop: Camden Town

In the mid-nineteenth century, Camden Lock hosted a gargantuan drinks complex, the Camden Goods Depot, owned by wine importers W&A Gilbey, which for a time was one of the largest drinks firms in the world. The site also included a large gin distillery. Today, it hosts a thriving open-air market popular with tourists and locals alike.

When he learned about this forgotten piece of drinks history, Camden native Mark Holdsworth was inspired to create his own gin, and founded the Half Hitch.

Half Hitch's two gins, the Earl Grey Tea Gin and Pink Berry Gin, take an unusual and time-consuming approach to production. The distillery itself blends spirits created through both pot still and vacuum still distillation in order to extract the most flavor possible from the botanicals: black tea, bergamot, pepper, hay, and wood. The gins' unusual colors are derived from using special tinctures that round out the sweetness.

The distillery hosts gin-making classes on most days where attendees can bring favorite botanicals to produce their own flavors.

HALF HITCH MARTINEZ

This is a strong version of the Martini's precursor, but allows the complexity of the gin to shine.

2 oz. Half Hitch Gin

¾ oz. Cocchi Torino

1 dash maraschino liqueur

Orange peel and Luxardo maraschino cherry, to garnish

1. Fill a mixing glass with ice and stir all the ingredients together.
2. Strain into a chilled coupette.
3. Garnish with the orange peel and cherry.

HAYMAN'S GIN

8A Weir Rd, London, SW12 0GT
Nearest Tube stop: Clapham South

Making gin since 1863, the Hayman family is gin royalty. They are direct descendants of James Burroughs, godfather of British gin distilling, who helped create what is now known as dry gin and founded the brand that eventually evolved into gin giant Beefeater.

In 1987, after a successful career working in the family business, Burroughs's great grandson, Christopher Hayman, struck out on his own and launched a variety of gin brands. Hayman's Gin first came to life in 2004 when his children, James and Miranda, joined the business to launch a gin liqueur. Eventually, the brand became a full-fledged distillery after a still was installed in 2013 in the family's Witham plant, just four miles away from Burroughs's original 1863 distillery site.

There are now many Hayman's gins available, some still based on nineteenth-century recipes, and the distillery runs tours and cocktail masterclasses for those willing to make the trek deep into the southwest outskirts of London.

HAYMAN'S LONDON MULE

This is a simple and refreshing cocktail that can be enhanced with your choice of bitters.

1 ¾ oz. Hayman's London Dry Gin

⅔ oz. fresh lime juice

5 oz. ginger beer

2 dashes bitters (optional)

Lime wedge, to garnish

1. Fill a cocktail mug (or highball glass) with ice and pour in the gin and lime juice before topping up with the ginger beer.

2. Add bitters, if desired, and garnish with a lime wedge.

TEMPLE BREW HOUSE

46 Essex St, London, WC2R 3JF
Nearest Tube stop: Temple

The Temple Brew Bar packs a lot of greatness into a small, unassuming basement, featuring a simple setup of wooden furniture, metal light fixtures, and exposed brick.

First, there is the beer. In addition to the superb range of constantly changing brews made at the on site microbrewery—all produced by head brewer Vanessa de Clac—there is a rotation of guest craft beers available on tap and to buy by the bottle, too.

Then there's the food, a cosmopolitan take on hearty brewpub fare that includes chicken kebabs, pulled pork quesadillas, kimchi-loaded Korean chicken burgers, and old-fashioned beef pies.

Finally, there's darts. One of the most beloved casual British sports, two serious interactive oches set up here are always in use.

It's unusual to find a venue like this, and of such good quality, in central London. That's why the bar is often full, so advance reservations are highly recommended.

ORBIT BEERS BREWERY & TAPROOM

233 Fielding St, London, SE17 3HD
Nearest Tube stop: Kennington

Walworth Road is the principle artery of the Camberwell neighborhood, which is notable for its varied independent businesses, restaurants, and markets. Just off of Walworth, under railway arches, you'll find the Orbit Beers Brewery. Its taproom showcases a wide array of brews, all made on site, and opens to a beer garden with plenty of space that backs onto the neighboring Pelier Park.

Orbit describes its beers as rooted in European tradition with a modern approach, and its core range features a pale ale, Belgian pale, a lager, and a porter. More experimental brews are on regular rotation.

There's also plenty going on. In addition to board games and a beanbag corner with Nintendo 64 consoles, there's a weekly pub quiz and a monthly bring-your-own-vinyl session where punters get a free pint in exchange for a 20-minute DJ session, in addition to many collaborations with local businesses and restaurants.

The Bermondsey Beer Mile

A legendary London beer crawl of local breweries in Bermondsey that happen to be operating right next to each other, the Bermondsey Beer Mile (which is closer to two miles) can only really be fully undertaken on a Saturday when all the breweries and taprooms in the neighborhood are open for business. Start with breakfast at the charming Maltby Market, and then get to work. Rather than being in alphabetical order, this is my suggested order for your beer-mile crawl.

SOUTHWARK BREWING
46 Druid St, SE1 2EZ

THE BARREL PROJECT/ LONDON BEER FACTORY
80 Druid St, SE1 2HQ

HAWKES CIDER
86-92 Druid St, SE1 2HQ

HIVER BEERS
56 Stanworth St, SE1 3NY

BREW BY NUMBERS
75 Enid St, SE16 3RA

BIANCA ROAD BREW CO
83-84 Enid St, SE16 3RA

CRAFT BEER JUNCTION
86 Enid St, SE16 3RA

THE KERNEL BREWERY
Arch 11, Dockley Road Industrial Estate,
Dockley Rd, SE16 3SF

SPARTAN BREWERY
8 Almond Rd, SE16 3LR

PARTIZAN BREWING
34 Raymouth Rd, SE16 2DB

FOURPURE BREWING CO.
25 Rotherhithe New Rd, SE16 3LL

JENSEN'S GIN

55 Stanworth St, London, SE1 3NY
Nearest Tube stop: Bermondsey

Danish national Christian Jensen was always obsessed with gin, and during a tasting session in Tokyo 20 years ago he realized how gin from previous decades far surpassed modern expressions. So he decided to take on gin as a side hustle to his day job, at a time when vodka was king.

After first working with British gin maestro Charles Maxwell to recreate a gin matching the "old-style" profile he was searching for, he founded Jensen's Gin while keeping up a full-time career as a finance IT professional.

Success enabled Jensen to build his own distillery and begin production in 2014. Sourcing botanical lists and distillation recipes from the past, he now oversees the production of two gins in the arches under a railway line—a London Dry and an Old Tom gin created from an 1840 recipe that he uncovered.

Situated in Jensen's longtime neighborhood of Bermondsey and surrounded by independent food and drinks businesses, the gin is now used in some of the world's best bars.

GREEN PARK

Jensen's Gin Distillery's official Old Tom gin cocktail
was created by former head bartender of the American Bar at the
Savoy, Erik Lorincz. Based on a White Lady, the herbal additions
help create a more complex drink.

2 basil leaves

1 ½ oz. Jensen's Old Tom Gin

1 oz. fresh lemon juice

½ oz. simple syrup

3 drops Bittermens Orchard Street Celery Shrub

2 teaspoons egg white

1. Slap the basil leaves to awaken the aromatics. Add them to a
   cocktail shaker along with ice and the remaining ingredients and
   shake vigorously, until chilled.

2. Strain into a coupe.

RENEGADE URBAN WINERY

Arch 12 Gales Gardens, London E2 0EJ
Nearest Tube stop: Bethnal Green

Tasting delicious local wines in a winery is not an experience you'd expect in the middle of London. But such is the dream realized by former asset manager Warwick Smith and winemaker Josh Hammond, who have been offering just that in the heart of London since 2016.

Renegade Wines in Bethnal Green ships in half its production grapes from European Union countries and the other half from within Great Britain. Smith and Hammond don't produce much by commercial standards—covering 12 to 14 wines and selling just 28,000 bottles a year across red, white, sparkling rosé, and even orange wines, and they are constantly experimenting with new blends and grape varietals.

At the end of each day, the winery, located under the railway arches of Bethnal Green station, closes and transforms into a candlelit bar, showcasing the fruit of its labor while also selling beer, cocktails, and food perfect for pairings. Indoors, the tables are placed next to the oak casks holding Renegade's wine, as well as the pumps and presses used for winemaking. The ample outdoor patio is surrounded by graffiti-covered walls, which, with the roar of the trains overhead, are an appropriate reminder that enjoying wine certainly doesn't have to imply snobbishness.

EAST LONDON LIQUOR COMPANY

Bow Wharf, Unit GF1, 221 Grove Rd,
London, E3 5SN
Nearest Tube stop: Bethnal Green

"**D**ecent booze for decent people at decent prices," is the mantra of this east London distillery. The booze is very decent indeed and the ELLC team is producing a variety of experimental gins, vodkas, and whiskies while also importing rum and American whiskey from California's superb Sonoma Distillery.

In addition to a single malt whisky matured in different casks, it was one of the first distilleries in the UK—and certainly the first in east London—to produce a rye whiskey. Its gins include a London Dry but also its Brighter Gin, which aims for spicy tannic notes, and its rich Louder Gin, which includes a floral hit of lavender. If you're not in the mood for hard spirits, the ELLC range of canned cocktails might float your boat.

The distillery, which also offers tours, has an excellent bar featuring its products and other spirits not produced by the distillery mixed into creative cocktails.

According to General Manager Siggi Sigurdsson, there's another fun fact about the bar that makes it stand out: "We have a distillery as a back bar. It's fitted with windows so you can see the still working while you get your drink on. It also symbolizes our commitment to transparency because we have nothing to hide."

EAST LONDON LIQUOR COMPANY BOULEVARDIER

This classic recipe (a Boulevardier is a Negroni that uses whisky or cognac instead of gin) uses the ELLC's rye whisky to add some real punch.

1 ½ oz. East London Liquor Company London Rye Whisky

1 oz. Campari

1 oz. sweet vermouth

Orange peel, to garnish

1. Add all of the ingredients to a mixing glass with ice, stir, and strain into a rocks glass filled with ice.

2. Garnish with the orange peel.

TAXI SPIRIT COMPANY

Haven Mews, Arch 412, St. Paul's Way,
London, E3 4AG
Nearest Tube stop: Mile End

After an intense period of time learning about brewing and distillation, while also driving his cab and raising four children, Moses Odong decided to plunge into distillation with his wife, Bianca. Taxi Spirits—guess the derivation of the name—is London's first white rum distillery, a small operation with a soundtrack provided by the rumbling trains passing overhead on their way to Mile End station.

Unlike many rums, which are often sweetened and colored, Taxi's white rum is produced from cane molasses without using any additional ingredients. The distillery also offers a spiced rum and even a gin, the result of an accident gone right after trying to create a recipe for the former. Production is small scale, with only 250 bottles of spirit produced from each batch distillation.

A tour at the distillery will allow you to try the full range of Taxi's spirits, and to see its column-still named after Odong's beloved sister, Irene, in action.

CABBY'S HEMINGWAY DAIQUIRI

Taxi's flagship cocktail for its white rum, this is a well-known variation on a classic Daiquiri.

2 oz. Cabby's White Rum

1 oz. fresh lime juice

¾ oz. grapefruit juice

¾ oz. demerara sugar syrup

¾ oz. maraschino liqueur

4 dashes grapefruit bitters

Lime wedge, to garnish

1. Combine all of the ingredients in a cocktail shaker with ice, shake well, and strain into a chilled coupette.

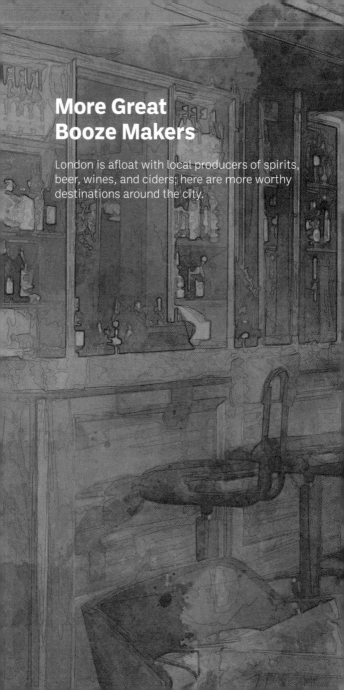

More Great Booze Makers

London is afloat with local producers of spirits, beer, wines, and ciders; here are more worthy destinations around the city.

58 AND CO
329 Acton Mews, E8 4EF

BEEFEATER
20 Montford Pl, SE11 5DE

BRICK BREWERY
209 Blenheim Grove, SE15 4QL

CITY OF LONDON DISTILLERY
22-24 Bride Ln, EC4Y 8DT

DOGHOUSE DISTILLERY
Unit L, London Stone Business Estate,
Broughton St, SW8 3QR

GOSNELLS OF LONDON
Bellenden Road Business Centre, Arches 1 & 2,
Bellenden Rd, SE15 4RF

HOWLING HOPS TANK BAR
Unit 9A Queen's Yard, White Post Ln, E9 5EN

LONDON BEER LAB
Arch 41, Railway Arches, Nursery Rd, SW9 8BP

LONDON CRU
21-27 Seagrave Rd, SW6 1RP

PORTOBELLO BREWING COMPANY
6 Mitre Way, W10 6AU

SACRED SPIRITS
50 Highgate High St, N6 5HX

Truth be told, London is filled with countless first-rate bars. The following are well worth a visit whether you are a local or visiting from elsewhere.

BATTERSEA AND CLAPHAM

Aspen & Meursault
96 Westbridge Rd, SW11 3PH
A classy wine shop and café with a focus on natural wines.

The Clapham Tap
128 Clapham Manor St, SW4 6ED
Board games, darts, ping-pong, great cocktails, and beer. What more could you want?

The Fox and Hounds
66-68 Latchmere Rd, SW11 2JU
A family-friendly sports-oriented pub with pool and darts.

Girlfriend
40 Battersea Rise, SW11 1EE
A high-quality cocktail bar with a pink theme.

Humble Grape Battersea
2 Battersea Rise, SW11 1ED
A wine bar highlighting sustainably produced wines.

The King and Co
100 Clapham Park Rd, SW4 7BZ
A pub with stripped-back décor and lots of craft beer.

Room 43
43 Lavender Hill, SW11 5QW
A locally loved bar that doubles as a Persian restaurant and jazz venue.

SIXTY | FOUR
64 Clapham High St, SW4 7UL
A wonderful bar made even better by a very generous happy hour policy.

The Victoria
166 Queenstown Rd, SW8 3QH
Lovely gastropub prioritizing real ales.

WC Wine and Charcuterie
Clapham Common South Side, SW4 7AA
A former public bathroom has been repurposed into a
wine and cocktail bar.

BRIXTON

Bar Marino
413 Brixton Rd, SW9 7DG
Top quality Italian food accompanied by top quality
cocktails.

Barrio Brixton
30 Acre Ln, SW2 5SG
South American food with a matching cocktail menu.

The Beast of Brixton
89 Acre Ln, Brixton Hill, SW2 5TN
A combination café/bar/workspace/wine bar/chicken
rotisserie.

The Effra Hall Tavern
38 Kellett Rd, SW2 1EB
A really lovely gastropub with excellent food, beers,
cocktails, and garden patio.

The Grosvenor Arms
17 Sidney Rd, SW9 0TP
A proper Victorian bar in the heart of Brixton.

The Junction
171 Coldharbour Ln, SE5 9PA
Live music is on six days of the week along with a great
tapas menu.

The Shrub and Shutter
336 Coldharbour Ln, SW9 8QH
This cocktail bar also doubles as a restaurant specializing in British cuisine.

Taproom by Brixton Village
Unit 43, 44 Coldharbour Ln, SW9 8PR
This taproom proudly showcases a wide variety of local beers.

Upstairs at the Ritzy
Chaplin House, Brixton Oval, SW2 1JG
The upstairs bar and venue of the Ritzy cinema.

The Whiskey Tumbler
401 Coldharbour Ln, SW9 8LQ
A very good Irish-themed cocktail bar.

CAMBERWELL AND PECKHAM

Beer Rebellion
129 Queen's Rd, SE15 2ND
Craft beer and ale specialists.

The Camberwell Arms
65 Camberwell Church St, SE5 8TR
A superb pub that also hosts comedy nights.

The CLF Art Lounge and Roof Garden
Station Way, SE15 4RX
A lush roof garden bar that also serves Dominican food.

Forza Wine
The Rooftop, 133A Rye Ln, SE15 4BQ
Great wines and a stellar view of the city.

Four Quarters
187 Rye Ln, SE15 4BN
Craft beers and ales are paired with retro arcade games.

Louie Louie
347 Walworth Rd, SE17 2AL
One of Camberwell's best cocktail bars features rotating guest chefs.

The Pigeon—Anspach & Hobday
41 Camberwell Church St, SE5 8TR
A craft beer bar and bottle shop that is also serious about wine and cocktails.

Stormbird
25 Camberwell Church St, SE5 8TR
An excellent pub focusing on craft ales from around the world.

Two Hundred Rye Lane
200 Rye Ln, SE15 4NF
A very, very good neighborhood cocktail bar.

Zapoi Bar
138 Rye Ln, SE15 4RZ
Enjoy a tasty vegan cocktail surrounded by enormous houseplants.

CAMDEN

All About Eve
31 Jamestown Rd, NW1 7DB
A charming neighborhood cocktail bar featuring weekly cabaret performances.

The Black Heart
3 Greenland Pl, NW1 0AP
Camden's best live punk and rock bar.

The Blues Kitchen
111-113 Camden High St, NW1 7JN
Live blues goes very well with the excellent selection of beer and whisky.

BYOC Camden
11-13 Camden High St, NW1 7JE
Bring your own bottles of booze and the bartenders here will make a tasty cocktail with them.

Camden Beer Hall
55-59 Wilkin Street Mews, NW5 3ED
This neighborhood brewery also has a small taproom where you can try a variety of lagers and pale ales.

Green Note
106 Parkway, NW1 7AN
A superb live music venue with a great selection of
drinks.

Hawley Arms
2 Castlehaven Rd, NW1 8QU
A locally loved gastropub that hosts live music.

Ladies and Gentlemen
2 Highgate Rd, NW5 1NR
A converted public toilet now serves very tasty sustainability oriented cocktails.

The World's End
174 Camden High St, NW1 0NE
A renowned pub and music venue that also serves excellent pizzas.

CHELSEA

Azteca
329 King's Rd, SW3 5ES
A Mexican cantina serving tasty Margaritas, Latin American food, and live music.

Bart's
Chelsea Cloisters, Sloane Ave, SW3 3DW
One of Chelsea's best cocktail bars.

Beaufort House
354 King's Rd, SW3 5UZ
A European bistro that has its own Champagne bar.

The Chelsea Pensioner
358 Fulham Rd, SW10 9UU
The best pub for watching a Chelsea FC football match.

Kona Kai
515 Fulham Rd, SW6 1HD
Southwest London's best tiki bar.

The Steam Packet
85 Strand-on-the-Green, Chiswick, W4 3PU
This riverside pub boasts a great selection of craft beer.

DALSTON

40FT Brewery and Taproom
2-3 Abbott St, London E8 3DP
This microbrewery and taproom is housed within a
shipping container.

Acqua7
7 Balls Pond Rd, N1 4AX
One of the area's best wine bars.

Brilliant Corners
470 Kingsland Rd, E8 4AE
The sound system and tunes are considered as important as the drinks.

High Water
23 Stoke Newington Rd, N16 8BJ
This tiny bar serves superb cocktails while also stocking
a serious selection of wines.

MAP Maison
321 Kingsland Rd, E8 4DL
Excellent cocktails and an extensive whisky list.

The Railway Tavern N16
2 St Jude St, N16 8JT
This nineteenth-century pub prides itself on its pints
and vegan pizza.

Ridley Road Market Bar
49 Ridley Rd, E8 2NP
A café during the day transforms into a tropical-themed
bar and club at night.

Servant Jazz Quarters
10A Bradbury St, N16 8JN
SJQ puts on loads of live music while also boasting
great cocktails.

Silk Stockings
80A Dalston Ln, E8 3AH
A tiny cocktail bar that prides itself on its hip-hop playlist.

TT Liquor
17B Kingsland Rd, London E2 8AA
A liquor store that also serves as a cocktail bar hosting all kinds of tastings and classes.

GREENWICH

Anchor and Hope
Riverside, SE7 7SS
A lovely pub with outdoor tables right by the Thames.

Meantime Brewing Company
Lawrence Trading Estate, Blackwall Ln, SE10 0AR
An award-winning local craft brewery.

Le Bar a Vin
72 Tranquil Vale, Blackheath Village, SE3 0BN
A local wine bar with a 100+ bottle list.

The Old Joinery
Ravensbourne Wharf, Norman Rd, SE10 9QF
A bar installed in a brick warehouse offering local beers, cocktails, and live music.

Oliver's Jazz Bar
9 Nevada St, SE10 9JL
One of southeast London's best jazz bars.

The Pelton Arms
Pelton Rd, SE10 9PQ
An old-school pub putting on live music, with one of the city's few bar billiards tables.

Plume of Feathers
19 Park Vista, SE10 9LZ
Founded in 1691, this is the oldest pub in Greenwich and a locally-revered institution located right next to the famous Greenwich Observatory.

The Prince of Greenwich
72 Royal Hill, SE10 8RT
An excellent Victorian pub hosting live music and a cinema club.

The River Ale House
131 Woolwich Rd, SE10 0RJ
Proudly labeling itself as a "microbpub," this award-winning pub manages to fit plenty of booze into its small space, especially beer and cider.

HACKNEY

Bar 161
161 Mare St, E8 3RH
Excellent cocktails and a generous happy hour policy.

Behind This Wall
411 Mare St, E8 1HY
Low-key basement bar creating bespoke cocktails and boasting a serious sound system.

Binch
51 Greenwood Rd, E8 1NT
Bottle shop and bar focusing on craft beers and natural wines.

Blondies
205A Lower Clapton Rd, Lower Clapton, E5 8EG
Local dive bar hosting gigs and serving great drinks.

The Gun
235 Well St, E9 6RG
Founded in 1860, this pub serves craft beer, artisan spirits, and has its own football team.

Helgi's
177 Mare St, E8 3RH
Burgers, hot dogs, cocktails, and hard rock bands. Nice.

The Kenton Pub
38 Kenton Rd, E9 7AB
One of Hackney's best-loved local pubs with an excellent quiz night, board games, and an enormous Norwegian moose head that serves as the pub mascot.

The Natural Philosopher
489 Hackney Rd, E2 9ED
A popular cocktail bar located inside a Mac repair shop.

NuDawn
206 Well St, London E9 6QT
A rum bar that also prides itself on its rotis and eclectic cultural events.

NOTTING HILL

The Act Bar
126-128 Notting Hill Gate, W11 3QG
A cocktail bar with plenty of theatrical flair; the servers double as performing artists throughout the evening.

Cépages Wine Bistro
69 Westbourne Park Rd, W2 5QH
A French-oriented tapas bar with plenty of wine on offer.

Electric Diner
191 Portobello Rd, W11 2ED
An American-style diner and bar part of a larger complex that includes a cinema.

Franklin's Wine
305 Westbourne Grove, W11 2QA
An excellent wine shop bar rapidly gaining attention since its 2020 opening.

The Ladbroke Arms
54 Ladbroke Rd, W11 3NW
One of Notting Hill's best-known local pubs.

The Mall Tavern
71 Palace Gardens Terrace, W8 4RU
A large Victorian gastropub with an excellent beer garden.

Monty
155 Westbourne Grove, W11 2RS
Monty showcases natural wines to pair with seasonal British cuisine.

Trailer Happiness
177 Portobello Rd, W11 2DY
Long-standing rum lounge and tiki bar, now a Notting Hill establishment.

When Abby Met Claud
24 Pembridge Rd, W11 3HL
A charming and kitsch restaurant that also makes great cocktails.

SOHO

Bar Américain
20 Sherwood St, W1F 7ED
An intimate art deco cocktail bar within the legendary Brasserie Zédel.

Bar Termini
7 Old Compton St, W1D 5JE
Possibly London's best Negroni, and the coffee is amazing, too.

Basement Sate
8 Broadwick St, W1F 8HN
The only food you can have alongside the top-quality cocktails are desserts.

Disrepute
4 Kingly Ct, Carnaby, W1B 5PW
A trendy basement cocktail lounge with leather booths that stays open late.

The French House
49 Dean St, London W1D 5BG
No laptops or phones allowed at this excellent wine bar/French restaurant.

Jack Solomon's
41 Great Windmill St, W1D 7NB
Speakeasy-themed bar with an extensive gin and whisky lists.

The London Gin Club
22 Great Chapel St, W1F 8FR
The name says it all. Over 100 gins available and plenty of gin cocktails, too.

Murder Inc.
36 Hanway St, W1T 1UP
An intimate basement cocktail bar styled like a Prohibition gangster's den.

Ronnie Scott's
47 Frith St, W1D 4HT
One of the world's best-known live music venues.

STOKE NEWINGTON

The Auld Shillelagh
105 Stoke Newington Church St, N16 0UD
Irish pub with live music nights and perfectly poured chilled Guinness.

The Axe
18 Northwold Rd, N16 7HR
A popular pub boasting 22 beers on tap.

Escocesa
67 Stoke Newington Church St, N16 0AR
Excellent tapas restaurant that offers well-priced oysters, great cocktails, Gin and Tonics, and sherry.

Lady Mildmay
92 Mildmay Park, N1 4PR
A locally loved gastropub with a strong selection of beer.

Loading Stoke Newington
129 Stoke Newington High St, N16 0PH
You can play computer, board, and video games for free while sipping on video game-themed cocktails.

Victory Mansion
18 Stoke Newington High St, N16 7PL
Cocktail bar serving superb Asian-themed tacos.

ACKNOWLEDGEMENTS

Though writing a book can be a lonely task, it can't happen without the support of many—and this one is no exception.

For my second project with Cider Mill Press I have to give a big thank you to my editor, Buzz Poole, for his flexibility and patience.

On the writing front, I'm enormously grateful to my father, David, for applying his decades of journalism experience when editing this book. My bandmate/business partner/friend/sometimes co-writer, Paul Archibald, was also invaluable with his help and research. My partner, Ania, also provided valuable feedback and infinite reserves of patience over the course of writing this book.

And finally, an enormous thank you to everyone working in London's hospitality and bar scene. This book is at its core a reflection of London's post-pandemic hospitality renaissance following a very hard couple of years. To see the city's amazing bars thriving once more is a true pleasure and privilege.

Felipe Schrieberg is a drinks writer, author, and musician.

He is a senior contributor to Forbes.com, for which he writes about whisky and the drinks industry, among many other global industry publications. He is also a judge for the World Whiskies Awards amongst other spirits competitions.

For his work, he has won the 2022 Icons of Whisky Communicator of the Year, the 2021 Alan Lodge Young International Drinks Writer of the Year, and was shortlisted for the Fortnum and Mason Drinks Writer of the Year and the IWSC Spirits Communicator awards.

A professional musician as a vocalist and lap steel guitarist, he is one-half of The Rhythm and Booze Project, which combines live music and whisky through gigs, tastings, and multimedia projects.

About Cider Mill Press
Book Publishers

Good ideas ripen with time. From seed to harvest, Cider Mill Press strives to bring fine reading, information, and entertainment together between the covers of its creatively crafted books. Our Cider Mill bears fruit twice a year, publishing a new crop of titles each spring and fall.

Visit us online at
cidermillpress.com

or write to us at
PO Box 454
12 Spring Street
Kennebunkport, Maine 04046